OUTSOURCING
A CIO's Perspective

by

Oakie Williams
Change Management Group
Jamestown, Ohio

S^t_L

St. Lucie Press
Boca Raton Boston London New York Washington, D.C.

OUTSOURCING
A CIO's Perspective

Library of Congress Cataloging-in-Publication Data

Williams, Oakie.
    Outsourcing : a CIO's perspective / by Oakie Williams.
         p. cm.
     Includes index.
     ISBN 1-57444-216-3 (alk. paper)
      1. Electronic data processing departments--Contracting out.
    2. Information resources management. I. Title.
    HF5548.2.W4678   1998
    658'.05--dc21   98-5000
                                                                  CIP

This book contains information obtained from authentic and highly regarded sources. Reprinted material is quoted with permission, and sources are indicated. A wide variety of references are listed. Reasonable efforts have been made to publish reliable data and information, but the author and the publisher cannot assume responsibility for the validity of all materials or for the consequences of their use.

Neither this book nor any part may be reproduced or transmitted in any form or by any means, electronic or mechanical, including photocopying, microfilming, and recording, or by any information storage or retrieval system, without prior permission in writing from the publisher.

The consent of CRC Press LLC does not extend to copying for general distribution, for promotion, for creating new works, or for resale. Specific permission must be obtained in writing from CRC Press LLC for such copying.

Direct all inquiries to CRC Press LLC, 2000 Corporate Blvd., N.W., Boca Raton, Florida 33431.

Trademark Notice: Product or corporate names may be trademarks or registered trademarks, and are only used for identification and explanation, without intent to infringe.

© 1998 by CRC Press LLC
St. Lucie Press is an imprint of CRC Press LLC

No claim to original U.S. Government works
International Standard Book Number 1-57444-216-3
Library of Congress Card Number 98-5000
Printed in the United States of America 1 2 3 4 5 6 7 8 9 0
Printed on acid-free paper

About the Author

Oakie Williams is the founder of the Change Management Group® (CMG), a management consulting and technology advisory firm specializing in providing Chief Information Officer outsourcing services as well as assisting companies in outsourcing their Information Technology-related responsibilities. For over 26 years, Mr. Williams has been working with companies and various government agencies to improve customer satisfaction, streamline operations, create revenue opportunities, and improve the quality of management information. Prior to forming CMG, Mr. Williams held many positions encompassing both line and staff assignments. This included executive positions such as Chief Information Officer (CIO) and Director of Business Process Improvement. As a CIO, he was responsible for the research, development, and maintenance of all voice, data, and imaging systems for a large manufacturing company in a global marketplace. Mr. Williams has introduced companies to new technologies and business solutions that enhanced the company's competitiveness and ensured they were aligned with business needs and organization change initiatives. Having been through the outsourcing process as an outsourcing provider and customer, Mr. Williams is well aware of the advantages and disadvantages associated with outsourcing Information Technology-related responsibilities.

With a strong background in business, Mr. Williams understands the significant challenges facing industry today and the delicate balance of blending Information Technology with business processes. His qualifications and experience include: Hands-on operations and business planning experience for diverse product lines in a multinational environment; served as a key member of several acquisition and divestiture initiatives; and a strong track record in the development of systems and business processes that increase productivity and efficiency. Mr. Williams' accomplishments include:

- B.S. in Business Administration
- M.A. in Business Administration and Management
- Certified in Production and Inventory Management (CPIM)
- Member of the University Of Dayton MIS Advisory Board
- Active member of the American Production and Inventory Control Society (APICS) and the American Manufacturing Excellence (AME) organization
- Veteran

Mr. Williams has written numerous white papers for organizations discussing the current and future state of various technologies and their impact on specific industries and organizational operations. In addition, he has authored several technical publications and has been a guest speaker for organizations such as the Information Technology Marketing and Sales Association (ITMSA), the New Zealand Production and Inventory Control Society (NZPICS), and numerous software user group conferences.

Acknowledgments

This book is dedicated to my family. Special thanks goes to my best friend and my life's companion, my wife. Without her support, encouragement, and assistance, I could not have achieved my personal and professional goals.

Contents

List of Illustrations

Introduction

In today's global competitive marketplace, the position of Chief Information Officer (CIO) has become a formidable link in the ranks of executive management in forward-thinking companies. Once thought of as "the senior computer guy," the position of Chief Information Officer has now become prestigious, recognized for its contribution to improving shareholder value and overall company improvement. Many senior executives have recognized the value that Chief Information Officers provide to a company. They are utilizing the opportunities to integrate Information Technology and business process improvement with the company's long-term strategic plan. Companies are also starting to realize that the position of Chief Information Officer can be used as a competitive advantage which strengthens its position in the global marketplace.

In this position, the Chief Information Officer is looked upon to recommend and oversee the implementation of business methods that add value and strengthen the company's strategic position. In this role, it is hard to imagine a Chief Information Officer who has not considered outsourcing as a viable alternative to improve his company's ability to utilize Information Technology (IT) and control costs. Once thought of as a business alternative for large companies, outsourcing has become a potentially viable business solution for any company serious about utilizing Information Technology to improve its strategic position, reduce cost, and improve quality. As a business entrepreneur, the Chief Information Officer realizes the business value of researching the possibilities of outsourcing. This does not mean that outsourcing is for everyone. Each specific environment — company attitude, technology position, current Information Systems (IS) organization, company strategic directions, corporate executive initiatives — will determine the feasibility of outsourcing. Until a company goes through the outsourcing evaluation, it will never know if outsourcing would be a good business decision.

Information Technology outsourcing is also rapidly becoming a major contributor to companies that are focusing their efforts on implementing supply chain management (SCM) solutions. As companies continue to take advantage of Information Technology to strengthen their competitive advantage, they are realizing the value Information Technology can have on their position in the market. Implementing supply chain management solutions allows companies all over the world to better control the flow of material between their customers and all levels of their supplier base. Information Technology outsourcing companies can greatly assist in the implementation of supply chain management by providing the technology and services needed throughout the supply chain. Many Information Technology outsourcing companies have already assisted many of their clients in implementing this business improvement solution. The larger outsourcing firms already have the Information Technology infrastructure in place that companies can use to reach their customers and suppliers.

Once the outsourcing alternative is reviewed, the majority of companies will find that it is an attractive business alternative and needs to be viewed as a potential for improvement, both in the Information Technology area and in other areas across the company. Today's outsourcing firms have broken out of the "glass house." Many of the larger outsourcing firms offer services that go far beyond the Information Technology organization. Areas such as business process improvement, customer service, finance, human resources, and other business functions can all be addressed with today's outsourcing firms. Once you have started the outsourcing evaluation, you will find that the real benefits of outsourcing are not limited to the Information Technology organization. Other areas of the company can realize benefits from outsourcing. When you think about it, the cost of Information Technology is usually in the range of 1 to 2% of sales. What about the other costs that account for much larger portions of the cost of sales?

Over the past 10 years, outsourcing firms have consistently demonstrated their abilities to successfully assume the responsibilities of Information Technology at a rate below that of a typical company. Today's outsourcing firms have also very successfully targeted the non-Information Technology business functions and are starting to build positive reputations with their abilities to effectively run non-Information Technology organizations. So when you talk about outsourcing today, you should be thinking on broader terms and not isolating the potential business value just to the Information Technology functional area.

After going through the outsourcing evaluation, the determination can be made as to whether or not outsourcing is a viable option for your company. Even if the decision not to outsource is reached, the result of the process will provide the Chief Information Officer and executive staff with potential business improvement opportunities. During the evaluation, the Chief Information Officer and the outsourcing firms will be evaluating the current usage of technology, the current Information Technology cost, company strategic focus, Information Technology personnel skill levels, and essentially all aspects of Information Technology in your company. The outsourcing firms, in turn, will be recommending their approach to improving your overall Information Technology environment. Regardless of your decision of whether or not to outsource, your company will benefit from the results of your efforts. If it is found that outsourcing is not the right alternative for your company, you will still have gained knowledge and various opinions from noted outsourcing experts. This experience will enable you to be a better Chief Information Officer and perhaps be in a position to take advantage of opportunities discovered during the outsourcing evaluation.

Following the evaluation, you will find your company is better informed and has a better appreciation for the types of things that can be done to improve the overall business process. While outsourcing certainly does not apply only to Information Technology, this book focuses on the process of outsourcing the Information Technology organization, often referred to as the Information Systems organization, and its responsibilities. It is up to each company, as it reviews outsourcing, to determine the applicability of outsourcing for areas other than Information Technology. You will find that once you have started the outsourcing process, it can be an enjoyable and enlightening experience. In my opinion, this should be a required exercise for all companies.

In today's business world you have to be tough and responsive to rapidly changing needs. Successful companies today are utilizing Information Technology to address these needs and strengthen their company's competitive position. Outsourcing has become a viable alternative to help strengthen the company and set the pace for competitors to follow.

This book addresses the advantages and disadvantages of outsourcing. It is up to each Chief Information Officer to determine if outsourcing is a good alternative for his or her specific company. To do so, each company will have to go through the exercises as outlined herein. This book is meant to invoke thought and provide possible strategies for the outsourcing process. It also addresses the realistic expectations and the common questions associated with outsourcing. If you are going to consider outsourcing, you need to know how to proceed through the outsourcing process. This book will guide you through the process and identify some of the hurdles typically associated with outsourcing. So keep an open mind, and while you may find that outsourcing is not the best approach for your company, who knows, you may just find that it is!

1 Why Outsource?

As global competition grows more fierce, companies continue to look for ways to increase their competitive edge without jeopardizing their profit margins. Today, corporations, large and small, are starting to realize the competitive advantage that Information Technology can bring to a company. These companies are also realizing that to stay current with technologies requires a great deal of effort, risk, and expense. This is one of the primary reasons why Chief Executive Officers and Chief Information Officers are considering outsourcing as an attractive alternative.

Regardless of all the positive reports you may hear about outsourcing, it is not for everyone. Companies that view Information Technology as a non-strategic function, or that have an annual Information Technology cost of less than 1% of sales, or are not willing to engage in a long-term partnership agreement will most likely not be successful in securing a profitable and manageable outsourcing agreement.

For companies that do not fit these criteria, it is most likely that an outsourcing agreement could be a viable alternative for their strategic direction. There are many reasons you may want to outsource. The reasons vary from one company to the next, but the majority of companies that already have outsourced see the major benefits of an outsourcing agreement as:

- Reduction of risk
- Center of expertise
- Taking advantage of future technologies
- Resource availability
- Information Technology professional growth
- Improved Information Technology customer service
- Cost savings

While these are just a few benefits for outsourcing, they are the areas in which any Board of Directors would be most interested. If a Chief Information Officer could effectively demonstrate that his or her company would benefit in each of the areas above, it is likely the Board of Directors would approve the recommendation to outsource. Let's take a closer look at each of the benefits.

Reduction of Risk

With any good outsourcing agreement, the outsource provider will share in the risks. The amount of risk an outsourcing firm will agree to assume will depend on the type of contract. For example, in a fixed-price contract the outsourcing firm will assume a great deal more risk than that of a time and material contract. Regardless of the type of contract, the one common denominator is that the Chief Information Officer will be sharing the responsibility for the future direction of the technology within his/her company with the outsourcer. It will still be the Chief Information Officer's responsibility to ensure the technology integration with business processes within the company. The outsourcer will (within the guidelines specified in the contract) assist by introducing new technologies and the personnel with the proper skills to implement them.

A properly structured outsourcing agreement will ensure the outsourcer assumes the appropriate risk. The outsourcer will have the responsibility to ensure the systems are meeting the reliability and performance criteria, ensuring that properly skilled personnel are available at the right time, and protecting your company from the "bleeding edge" of technology.

Center of Expertise

Since an outsourcing firm's primary business is to manage technology for clients, it is appropriate to assume they have experience with current, as well as new, technologies. Larger outsourcing firms embrace the "center of expertise" concept, in which a group of research and development technology engineers are dedicated to evaluating new products and their applicability throughout industry. The center of expertise concept is called by different names (e.g., center of excellence, skill centers, application specialist centers, competency centers, proficiency centers, etc.). Regardless of the title, the concept is the same: to have highly specialized personnel address new technologies and provide support for existing systems. As a result, when your company decides to evaluate a new technology, the outsourcing firm can supply experienced personnel to quickly evaluate the functional fit of the technology with the company's stated requirements. Even for the most technology-aggressive clients, it would be a challenge to find a new technology that the larger outsourcing firms had not already experienced. They most probably have a skilled workforce ready to assist their customers, regardless of the selected technology.

The center of expertise can also provide consulting services as well as hardware and software evaluations. By the very nature of its name, the center of expertise for consulting is made up of individuals highly specialized in specific fields, industries, and applications. These personnel could be utilized on a temporary basis to help solve issues and to facilitate the knowledge transfer to your company's development and service staff.

Taking Advantage of Future Technologies

As new technologies emerge, most companies cannot immediately take advantage of them because of the cost and learning curve associated with these technologies. Since one of the strategic initiatives for an outsourcing firm is to stay current with new technologies, they would be responsible for maintaining a high competency level in current, as well as new, technologies. As such, the outsourcer is in a position to provide experienced personnel and to assess the value of new application technologies. Since the outsourcing firm will be familiar with the new technologies, your company will spend less time, effort, and incur less risk in implementing the technologies.

The outsourcing firm will also assign an Account Manager to be the senior representative for its firm. This Account Manager will have profit and loss (P&L) responsibilities for the account. As such, he/she will be looking for opportunities to introduce new technologies within the company and generate additional business for the outsourcing firm. The Account Manager will also be in charge of the outsourcing account team.

The outsourcing account team consists of information system professionals from the outsourcing firm who are assigned to your company on a full- or part-time basis. The outsourcing account team will also be working daily with various managers and employees and be in a position to introduce new technologies where appropriate. The introduction of new technologies may or may not be within the scope of the contract, depending on how the contract is structured.

Once the opportunity for new technology implementation is identified, the outsourcing firm will most likely have the capability of implementing the technology on a trial basis to ensure the best possible solution. This again reduces the risk of your company investing in new technologies that may not be of value or meet your expected results. The larger outsourcing firms would also be in a position to introduce you to an established client who has already implemented the technology, thus providing you the opportunity to discuss the advantages and disadvantages of the new technology.

Regardless of the other reasons for outsourcing, the technology benefit is significant for companies who are on a fast pace and realizing significant growth. It is also beneficial for companies that have "lean" Information Technology budgets and cannot afford the trial and error associated with testing new technologies.

Resource Availability

As business needs change and customer demands fluctuate, the requirement for Information Technology resources will fluctuate as well. Outsourcing firms can provide additional professional resources on an as-needed basis. This reduces your cost of retaining permanent employees and/or utilizing industry consultants for short-term engagements. As a result, the outsourcer can guarantee the knowledge and experience level and ensure that the personnel is available when (and as long as) needed. Utilizing the personnel in the center of expertise areas, and the use of the help desk (or support center) concept, the outsourcing firm can often provide the necessary assistance from a remote location. The larger outsourcing firms have the ability to draw upon thousands of employees throughout the world on an as-needed basis. In the event the outsourcing firm does not have the skilled personnel available when needed, they also have the ability to contract with a third-party consulting firm to provide the necessary resources.

In a well-structured contract, the terms and pricing for this additional help will be identified so that your company is well aware of the cost for any additional assistance whether it be internal or external to the outsourcing firm.

Information Technology Professional Growth

The constant challenge that each company shares is the need to continuously challenge the internal Information Systems staff. The majority of industry today is in business to produce something other than Information Technology services. As a result, it is common to find situations where the internal Information Systems staff is not properly trained nor kept abreast of new technologies in their profession. The dilemma that faces each Chief Information Officer is how to keep the professional Information Systems staff current with technology, enthusiastic about their work, and institute a career path that will attract and retain the level of expertise required. In a time in which the competitive edge means being the low-cost provider for quality products, the training for staff personnel is often the first thing to be cut from a budget to reduce overhead costs. As a result, the Information Systems staff rarely receives the training necessary to continue to perform at maximum efficiency levels required to build a quality product and stay current with technologies.

Every outsourcing firm's revenue is heavily dependent upon the quality of service their personnel provides. As such, the outsourcers will typically invest a great deal more in training and education per person on Information Technology training and education compared to a nonoutsourcing firm. To illustrate the value of continued education, the outsourcing firm typically will reduce its cost by re-engineering the Information Technology processes within your company's Information Technology organization. This is done through innovative techniques and utilizing state-of-the-art tools.

Improved Information Technology Customer Service

It is often said: "The value of our products is only as good as our customer service department." The same is true for Information Technology. Having a great customer service relationship is as important as the quality and cost effectiveness of the products being produced and maintained. As with most professions, the systems being developed by Information Technology today are becoming more and more sophisticated and complex. At the same time, the knowledge level of the user community is increasing but not at the same rate. Therefore, it is imperative to establish and maintain an excellent help desk (support center) to provide a point of contact for the user community. While larger companies have an existing help desk, the outsourcing firm can often improve the effectiveness and response time through utilization of highly skilled technicians and appropriate tools. For companies that do not have a help desk, the outsourcer can either implement one on site or utilize their existing centralized help desk.

A properly structured contract will insist that the outsourcing firm utilize a state-of-the-art help desk function. This assumes that the outsourcing agreement includes transitioning the Information Technology employees. Regardless of the size of the contract, this is an area in which outsourcing firms do extremely well. They have the means, capability, and knowledge to establish and operate a first class help desk function.

Cost Savings

While most companies show significant reduction in cost when outsourcing, it should *not* be an automatic assumption. Many other factors contribute to the cost and savings of an outsourcing agreement:

1. Aggressiveness of the current Information Systems staff
2. Company size
3. Current Information Systems budget
4. Strategic direction of the company
5. Size of the Information Systems staff
6. Current computing architecture
7. Telecommunications business partners
8. Current hardware and software suppliers
9. Hardware and software maintenance agreements
10. Lease and contractual obligations, etc.

While outsourcing firms can provide a savings in many areas, the primary reason for these savings is their ability to take advantage of economies of scale. Since outsourcing firms are providing the same type of service for literally hundreds (and sometimes thousands) of customers, they are able to consolidate data center operations, which provides lower overhead costs on a per-customer basis. They are also in a position to receive deep discounts from hardware and software suppliers because of their annual volume of business. The larger outsourcing firms also provide the added benefit of acting as your aggregator for telecommunications networking and cost reduction. Again, this is due to the size and volume of business resulting from the consolidation of multiple clients.

Another area in which outsourcing firms can provide savings is within the Information Systems organization itself. The personnel in the information systems organization typically spends the majority of their time maintaining and re-engineering applications for their company. It is often said, "Information Systems organizations have automated all functional areas within their companies...except their own." Rarely is the process re-engineering focused on the Information Systems organization. Outsourcing firms apply state-of-the-art tools and lessons learned from hundreds of accounts to improve the process flows and efficiencies of the Information Systems organization. Doing so results in improved efficiencies and cost reductions. This is the only way an outsourcing firm can realize a savings in Information Systems personnel costs. Generally speaking, the rate of pay for their employees is higher than that of the client to which they are outsourcing. As a result, they must, and quite effectively do, increase output and efficiencies to control their personnel costs.

While there are no guarantees, a general rule of thumb is that, as a result of outsourcing, your company should realize a 10 to 30% Information Systems-related savings over a 10-year period. The trend in the Information Systems industry points to a higher percentage of savings in the higher Information Technology budgets. Companies with very lean Information Technology budgets (less than 1.2% in sales) will find it difficult to realize a savings by outsourcing. Even when there are no cost savings, outsourcing may still be the best solution for the company. Cost is only one of many factors on which to base the decision to outsource. For example, a company may have an overwhelming need to take advantage of advanced technologies and will be willing to pay a higher price to achieve that goal.

A fact to remember is that while there are many advantages to outsourcing, it is not necessarily the right decision for all companies. Each Chief Executive Officer and Chief Information Officer must assess the advantages of outsourcing for his/her specific organizations.

When investigating the outsourcing alternative, you should develop an Outsourcing Model. This model could consist of the various high-level steps required during the outsourcing process. For your consideration, a suggested Outsourcing Model is provided in Figure 1.1. This model contains the major activities required for a thorough requirements definition, evaluation, and implementation of a typical outsourcing partnership.

At a minimum, you should include each step of the model to ensure that you do not overlook an important phase of the process. You may want to add additional steps to the model to fit your specific needs. After developing your own version of the Outsourcing Model, use it as a guideline throughout the outsourcing process. It can also be used as a means of communicating the progress you and the Outsourcing Team are making. The Outsourcing

```
┌─────────────────────────────────────────┐
│                                          │
│    1.  Establish The Need                │
│                                          │
│    2.  Develop The Outsourcing Strategy  │
│                                          │
│    3.  Develop The Cost Model            │
│                                          │
│    4.  Develop The Request For Proposal  │
│                                          │
│    5.  Selection Of The Winning Proposal │
│                                          │
│    6.  Determine Risks                   │
│                                          │
│    7.  Contract Development              │
│                                          │
│    8.  Contract Negotiations             │
│                                          │
│    9.  Transition Responsibilities       │
│                                          │
│   10.  Manage The Partnership            │
│                                          │
└─────────────────────────────────────────┘
```

Figure 1.1   The Outsourcing Model

Team is a group of individuals from your company who are assigned the task of assessing the viability of outsourcing, developing a request for proposal, selecting the proper outsourcing firm, and structuring and negotiating the final agreement with the outsourcing firm. As you refine your model, you should start to break each step down to the lowest level possible. This way, you will have your own checklist to ensure that you do not overlook any part of the process.

2 Developing an Outsourcing Strategy

Once you determine outsourcing to be a viable alternative, you should develop a strategy to determine how best to proceed. Developing a good strategy is one of the single most important steps in the process. The strategy must be developed at the senior executive level, usually at the Chief Executive Officer and/or Chief Information Officer level. This would involve decisions pertaining to the level of outsourcing a company would want to pursue. For example, many companies that have outsourced have included all Information Systems activities, while others have only outsourced a portion of them. Great care should be taken to ensure that only those portions of the business that make the most sense in terms of benefits, risk, and cost are considered for outsourcing. A faulty strategy will result in a no-win situation for you and/or the outsourcing firm, which can potentially cause a great deal of hardship for both parties, resulting in a waste of time, effort, and cost.

To effectively develop a good outsourcing strategy will require a great deal of research. With the amount of money and the number of issues involved in a typical outsourcing agreement, I would advise you to retain outside consulting assistance for building the outsourcing strategy. The long-term benefits and potential savings far outweigh the short-term cost of retaining a consultant. The consultant would also work closely with the designated personnel to further define the pros and cons of outsourcing and inform you of any potential problems that may be on the horizon.

Since developing the outsourcing strategy is a crucial exercise, you should seek the advice and experience of others. As mentioned above, conferring with a consultant is certainly a viable option, but in addition to that, you should also talk with other companies who have already completed the outsourcing exercise. The outsourcing firms themselves are also an excellent source of information to help evaluate the best outsourcing strategy. Let's assess the value-added from all three sources of information — a consultant, outsourcing firms, and companies that have already gone through the outsourcing process.

Consultant

Consulting services should be sought in the early stages of developing the strategy. There are many consulting firms in industry today that specialize in outsourcing. Due to the significant growth and increased interest in outsourcing, many consulting firms realize the potential for added business and are building expertise in outsourcing areas. The consulting firm should not be from a company that actually provides outsourcing services. This will prevent the possibility of obtaining biased directions and opinions. Selecting the consultant should be a well-thought-out decision. While there are many large consulting firms that deal with outsourcing, it does not necessarily mean that larger is better. There are many small consulting companies in today's environment that provide quality assistance.

It is important to select an individual or company you feel comfortable with. You must be confident they have experience in the outsourcing arena and the proper understanding of your business. Remember, you are not necessarily looking for someone who will actually implement or transition your company to an outsourcing firm, but rather someone who can work with your senior management to assess the best possible strategic direction for your company. Once the decision has been made on who the consulting individual will be, this individual will assist you in developing an outsourcing strategy that will maximize your efforts, profits, and shareholder value. You may decide to retain the consultant throughout the entire outsourcing process. This, of course, depends on the quality of the value-added services the consultant provided during the outsourcing strategy definition phase of the project. Selecting a consultant is discussed in detail in Chapter 10, "When To Use Consultants."

Outsourcing Firms

Another method to assist you in developing an outsourcing strategy is talking with the outsourcing firms themselves. Since outsourcing firms have experience with many types of outsourcing contracts, they are an excellent source for obtaining the information required to develop your strategy. The outsourcing firm's marketing representatives will be happy to meet with you and discuss the various benefits and options associated with outsourcing. They, along with the consultant you have selected, can provide a multitude of information to help assess the proper strategy for your company. Use caution not to get too many people from outside your company involved. It is wise to limit the discussions to no more than three or four different outsourcing firms. It is important that, as you initiate the conversations, you tell them you are in a data-gathering mode to help develop your outsourcing strategy. At that point, each outsourcing firm will most probably try to convince you to sole-source your business. But, beware! This may not be the most beneficial way to award the contract. This is discussed further in Chapter 4, "Request For Proposals."

Companies That Have Already Gone Through the Outsourcing Process

Talk with your peers at other companies who have already outsourced. There is no teacher like experience. Companies that have already been through the outsourcing activity are excellent sources of information. They are in a position to thoroughly inform you as to what went right, what went wrong, and why. Even though each outsourcing agreement is unique and at times cannot be compared to any other outsourcing case, the approach and activities required to develop an outsourcing agreement are the same. Those who have already been through this activity are by far in the best position to provide advice to anyone contemplating outsourcing. If you are not aware of anyone who has been through the outsourcing activity, this information can be obtained in many ways.

First, the outsourcers would be happy to provide references. Care should be taken with an outsourcer reference. It is highly unlikely the outsourcer will provide a reference for an account that is not in good graces with the outsourcer and has had anything less than an excellent relationship with them. We all know that there is no such thing as a 100% happy customer. Regardless of who the outsourcer is, I can assure you there are cases in which the outsourcing agreement has not been as successful and positive as they had hoped.

Another way of finding companies that have already outsourced is through your consultant. The consultant will have many contacts in this area and should be happy to share them with you. Trade shows and conferences are also an excellent place to obtain this type of information. By networking with your peers at conferences you will be able to obtain information about specific questions you may have.

The key to developing a good outsourcing strategy is obtaining the information necessary to educate and inform your executive staff. Remember, a good outsourcing strategy is crucial. This is not the place, nor the time, to take shortcuts or try to save a few dollars. This is the area, however, to take the time necessary and spend the appropriate money on travel, conferences, literature, and consulting to ensure the strategy is the very best for your company.

While developing the outsourcing strategy, the Chief Information Officer must remember that each outsourcing agreement is structured for each specific company and is unlikely to fit the needs of a second company. Therefore, there is no recipe for a successful outsourcing strategy. It must be developed by each individual company. Typically, an outsourcing firm will target the total Information Technology responsibilities within a company. These include:

1. Telecommunications
2. Data center operations
3. Applications development
4. Help desk
5. Training
6. Hardware support
7. Software support

Their strategy is most generally a common one: to persuade a client to include as much of the Information Technology responsibilities as possible. While they may agree to start with a portion of the responsibilities (such as data center operations), the outsourcing firm's long-term goal is to increase its market share by growing the existing business as well as retaining new clients. There is nothing wrong with this strategy. An outsourcing firm is like any other company. They are in business to make money, and to do so they must increase their market share, control their costs, and increase their margins. With this in mind, you should have a solid outsourcing strategy that has been tested and verified by an industry expert as being a sound strategy. It is important for the outsourcing committee (discussed in Chapter 3, "Forming a Partnership") to have a good understanding of their own strategy and the outsourcing firm's strategies prior to starting the contract negotiating process.

When developing the outsourcing strategy, a few key questions must be asked. The answers will help form the guidelines to develop a clear and concise outsourcing strategy.

1. Are you confident that you currently have a good Information Technology business plan and strategy?
2. Is your current Information Technology strategy integrated with the company's long-term business plan?
3. What is the current Information Technology cost of the company in terms of percentage of sales, as compared to your specific industry average?
4. Are your systems current with today's technologies?
5. Are you convinced the current systems are meeting your current requirements?
6. What is the general method for annual training of Information Technology personnel?
7. Do you feel the knowledge and training level of your Information Technology personnel is adequate to address your needs today and in the future?
8. What is your competition doing in the area of technologies?
9. Do you have a centralized or decentralized Information Technology organization?
10. Would you want to include all aspects of Information Technology in an outsourcing agreement? If so, why?
11. Are your systems wholly owned, leased, financed, or a combination? What is the value in each category?
12. Do you have good documentation supporting the hardware/software maintenance agreements with your current suppliers? What is their position on allowing an outsourcing firm to assume responsibility for the equipment?
13. Are all of your business units utilizing a common data communications network, i.e., Wide Area Network?
14. Is voice communications management an issue?
15. What is the level of computer sophistication among the user community within your company?
16. Are you utilizing a mainframe processor?

17. If your company has multiple business units, will you require them to use common Information Systems?
18. Do you have an existing business recovery plan?
19. Is your Chief Information Officer capable of objectively conducting the outsourcing process and managing it in the event an agreement is reached with an outsourcing firm?
20. Has your company had experience with outsourcing other portions of the business? If so, what were the results and lessons learned?

The answers to these questions should help you assess the type of outsourcing that would best suit your needs. While developing your outsourcing strategy keep the areas in mind that you feel will present the greatest challenges in the future. These areas are prime candidates for outsourcing.

There are literally thousands of variations of strategies that a company can develop. When one thinks about the number of tasks a typical Information Technology organization does year after year, it becomes a significant challenge to assess what should be included in an outsourcing agreement and what should be retained by the company. One would think that outsourcing everything realted to Information Technology would be the easiest of all scenarios, but this may not be the case. When developing a strategy, there are no right or wrong answers, just different approaches.

Good indicators for starting to develop a strategy would be the strengths and weaknesses of your current Information Technology direction and strategic focus. For example, if your focus was to consolidate data centers and to reduce Information Systems expenses, re-engineering the Information Technology business processes may be a good candidate for a total outsourcing arrangement. However, if you feel confident that your applications development and overall Information Technology strategic focus was a good approach, the company may want to look at only outsourcing the operations or network management responsibilities. Either way, both scenarios have their advantages and disadvantages. The following section illustrates the primary differences between full outsourcing and partial outsourcing.

Full Outsourcing

By definition, full outsourcing implies that all current Information Technology responsibilities will be outsourced. This would include: data center operations, telecommunications, applications development, training, help desk, maintenance, hardware configuration and control, document control, etc. Typically, the assumption is: with full outsourcing, all Information Systems personnel and management (with the exception of the Chief Information Officer) are transitioned to the outsourcer. In reality, this is not the case. A company will still need Information Systems expertise to help with technology integration throughout the company and provide an interface with the outsourcer.

Information Systems personnel are also retained for helping to assess the performance and daily management of the outsourcing account team. A rule of thumb for assessing the number of Information Systems personnel that should be retained is: one person for every $3 million of annual Information Technology-related expense. Besides personnel, there are other Information Technology-related expenses that you would retain. Expenses such as taxes, insurance premiums, depreciation (assuming the depreciated hardware was not transitioned to the outsourcer), amortization, and others would most likely be retained by the company because there is no value-added in transitioning the expenses or responsibilities to the outsourcer.

An advantage of full outsourcing is that all Information Technology personnel, with the exception of a select few, would be transitioned to the outsourcer. This would nearly eliminate problems that would naturally occur with a group of professionals working as peers with different professional opportunities, benefits, and career paths. Including all personnel in the transition provides the same opportunities and career growth potential for each individual. These and other personnel considerations are described in detail in Chapter 8, "Personnel Considerations."

There are three areas of concern for full outsourcing. One is the disadvantage of having to literally turn over the "keys to the kingdom" to an outside firm. Depending on senior management's opinion of the value of the internal Information Technology function, this may or may not be a valid strategy. The outsourcing firm becomes your partner in business. It is not to be considered a supplier relationship. It is in the outsourcer's best interest to ensure the success of the relationship. While this minimizes the risk of turning over total control of the company's information to an outsourcing firm, it does not negate the fact that the company no longer has total control of its own information. At the opposite end of the spectrum, full outsourcing provides the outsourcer with increased opportunities for success. They will have a larger base to work from in terms of cash, personnel, and overall freedom to make the necessary changes to reduce their risk and add value to your organization.

The second largest disadvantage involving full outsourcing is the added complexity of transitioning the Information Technology responsibilities back to the company at some point in the future. When developing the outsourcing strategy, you must assume that at some point in time, though it may be 10 to 15 years in the future, you will no longer need the services of an outsourcing firm. At that time it would be desirable to transition the Information Technology responsibilities back to the company and end the relationship with the outsourcing firm. With an outsourcing strategy focused on full outsourcing, you must face the fact that one day everything that is being done during the initial transition will have to be done in reverse.

The risk at that point is that you may or may not own the hardware and software you are using to run your business. In addition, the personnel that knows the most about your critical business systems will not be your employees. Further, they will most likely not be the employees you transfer to the outsourcing firm. This constitutes a significant risk since there are no guarantees that the personnel working on the account would transition to your company.

This risk can be minimized by proper contract language stating that the outsourcing firm will give the current outsourcing account team employees the option to transition to the company. It is impossible for the outsourcer to guarantee that the employees will exercise this option. It will be up to the employees to make that decision on an individual basis.

The last significant disadvantage to full outsourcing is that it creates a much larger burden on the Outsourcing Team to initially identify all tasks that an outsourcing firm must do during the life of the contract. If you think this may not seem like a significant effort, write down everything you did over the last twelve months and everything you think you will do over the next 10 years! It is extremely difficult to identify everything an organization does over a long period of time. This is further complicated by the fact that many things are done that are not documented. Right or wrong, there are no Information Technology organizations that can identify everything they do in clear, concise language that can just be handed over to an outsourcing firm. A way to minimize this risk is through the use of Service Level Agreements (SLA), defined in Chapter 4, "Request For Proposals," and other risk abatement methods further discussed in Chapter 5, "Proposal Evaluations."

Partial Outsourcing

Partial outsourcing implies that a company will identify a portion of the current responsibilities and look to an outsourcing firm to provide services

in those areas. Data center operations, network management, and telecommunication administration are three areas that are generally found in a partial outsourcing arrangement. Generally speaking, a partial outsourcing agreement is usually found in areas where the performance measurements are well defined and easily measured. Areas such as application development requires a higher skill level and increased management to ensure success of a partial outsourcing agreement. Many companies are reluctant to outsource their application development staff due to their knowledge of the business and their technical knowledge. Depending on specific instances, this may or may not be the case.

A definite advantage to partial outsourcing is that there will be a greater number of outsourcing firms from which to choose. There are many companies that deal with the operations network management that will not deal with applications development and other support services. Thus, for full outsourcing scenarios, these companies are not considered a competitor. In this light, the executive management must use caution. All outsourcing firms are not necessarily right for a specific company. It is like anything else — buyer beware. You have to find the firm that has a clear and distinct advantage over the others.

Partial outsourcing has the advantage of reduced risk associated with not having all Information Systems personnel transitioned to the outsourcing firm. The possibility of being understaffed with critical resources in the event of contract termination in the future is minimal. A significant advantage is the opportunity to test the waters before you form a long-term partnership with an outsourcing firm. This allows a company, and the outsourcing firm, to reach a comfort level before committing to a full outsourcing arrangement. A well-written contract will allow for renegotiation at any time.

This is a way, for a company concerned about the validity of the promises being made by outsourcing firms, to achieve the comfort level they need prior to committing greater amounts of the company's cash and giving the outsourcing firm additional responsibilities. Partial outsourcing would allow the outsourcing firm to build a positive relationship with the majority of the company's employees before the potential full outsourcing decision at a later date.

There are disadvantages to partial outsourcing. The outsourcing firm's lack of total control inhibits its ability to make dramatic improvements to your processes. When some personnel (but not all) are transitioned, you will inevitably cause a dispute between transitioned and nontransitioned employees at some point in the future. Partial outsourcing will increase the need for daily work assessments due to some tasks being completed by transitioned employees and some by nontransitioned employees.

The current organizational structure of an Information Systems organization will also determine if partial outsourcing is a viable alternative. If your company has a decentralized Information Systems organization, then what may be right for one section of Information Systems may not be good for another. A company may want to outsource one location instead of all locations. This strategy, however, should be carefully viewed for its impact on the total Information Systems organization when one organization will be treated differently than another. Generally speaking, partial outsourcing is usually found in smaller organizations. This is primarily because smaller companies have leaner budgets and overall tighter control than larger companies.

Developing an outsourcing strategy is key to the success of an outsourcing partnership. It is important to take the time to develop a strategy that is agreed upon throughout the executive management of the company and provides a value-added advantage that is linked to the strategic business plan. Timing is everything when considering an outsourcing arrangement. Clearly, it is best prior to a company going through technology refreshment or major systems upgrade. This would provide the outsourcing firm the opportunity to work with the company's senior management to define, design, and implement the next generation of systems that would meet the company's needs and allow the outsourcing firm to excel where its strengths are the greatest. On the opposite side, the least likely time to outsource is shortly after a large-scale systems upgrade. While it is not impossible to negotiate a favorable agreement with an outsourcing firm at that time, it is much more difficult. This is primarily because of fixed costs (depreciation, maintenance fees, etc.) the company has incurred during the new systems upgrade. A good time to outsource is when a company is growing via expansion: whether it be internal, by acquisition, by increasing market share, or buying the competition. These are times when one generally sees a significant increase in Information Technology costs and a company assumes a greater risk of locking into a technology that will hopefully best suit its needs. Outsourcing during these times will provide an opportunity for an outsourcing firm to share the risk of these major strategic decisions and also provide fixed costs for future planning.

It is also highly recommended to create an outsourcing committee. The purpose of the outsourcing committee is to function as the governing body and perform all required tasks throughout the outsourcing process. The outsourcing committee should be made up of senior executives who have the background and knowledge to:

1. Define the requirements of outsourcing
2. Have major input into the development of the request for proposal
3. Assess the value of each proposal received from each outsourcing firm
4. Determine if outsourcing is a viable alternative
5. Select the outsourcing firm that would best fit the company requirements
6. Negotiate the contract
7. Recommend and present to the Board of Directors (or appropriate management) for the final decision to outsource

The outsourcing committee should be limited in the number of members. By having a smaller group, the outsourcing committee will be more effective in reaching the decisions necessary to move forward. At a minimum, the committee members should be the Chief Information Officer, Chief Financial Officer (CFO) or Controller, Vice President of Manufacturing, and a company attorney.

The outsourcing committee is a working committee. As such, it should be prepared to spend many hours a week working as a group throughout the outsourcing process. It should be known and understood up front that the outsourcing committee members' calendars must be arranged so that they can commit the time necessary to adequately address the outsourcing process. Without this dedication and commitment from each of the outsourcing committee members, the outsourcing process will potentially be extended for many months longer than necessary. Or worse, they will fail in their mission to assess the potential business benefit of outsourcing.

3 | Forming a Partnership

D oing business with an outsourcer is not like any other customer/supplier relationship. Signing an agreement with an outsourcer means you are entering into a partnership with another company which both parties feel will be mutually beneficial. *The American Heritage Dictionary* defines partnership as: "A contract entered into by two or more persons (companies) which each agrees to furnish a part of the capital and labor for a business enterprise and by which each shares in some fixed proportions in profits and losses." The same is true for an outsourcing partnership. Both companies should be prepared to share in the profits and losses throughout the term of the contract.

The partnership is a means to collectively strengthen the weaknesses and capitalize on the strengths. The Chief Executive Officer and Chief Information Officer must understand that when entering into an agreement with an outsourcer, the outsourcer must make a profit. Otherwise, the outsourcing firm will not survive the long-term partnership.

When negotiating with an equipment supplier to purchase an item, the negotiations are conducted until the buyer feels comfortable that the price is the lowest possible price for the item being received. While negotiating with an outsourcer you certainly want to be assured you are getting the best price for the value of services that will be delivered. You also must keep in mind that the lower the outsourcer goes in price, the less money they will have to do the job that needs to be done. The negotiation process should continue in good faith, but understand that there is a definite point where lowering the price of the agreement will eventually start to deteriorate the quality of the services to be received. The Chief Executive Officer and the Chief Information Officer must determine where the appropriate cutoff point is and feel comfortable that when that point is reached they are getting the best value for the price being paid.

It is essential that at the end of the negotiation process both companies feel comfortable with the results. Otherwise, there is a strong probability that the partnership is headed for troubled times.

To ensure that the executive management of both companies stays involved in the partnership, I highly recommend forming an Information Technology Council to ensure that both the outsourcing firm and your company keep abreast of the direction of the relationship. This council would be responsibile for ensuring that major issues are resolved before they become significant problems. The Information Technology Council would also be responsible for ensuring the relationship maintains the enthusiasm and focus that was intended when the partnership began. It should also be established that any contract dispute would be reviewed by the Information Technology Council prior to arbitration.

The Information Technology Council would be made up of members of the executive staff from both companies. At a minimum, each company should have three representatives. The outsourcing firm's representatives would be the president of the appropriate business unit, the divisional or regional manager responsible for the account, and the Account Manager's direct supervisor. Your company's representation would also be made up of senior company executives. A sample of the representation would be the Chief Information Officer, Chief Financial Officer, and Vice President of Manufacturing.

The Information Technology Council should meet at least every six months. The meetings should be considered as an opportunity to review the current status of the partnership, resolve any open issues that have been escalated to the Information Technology Council, and establish and agree upon plans and specific actions for the future. In effect, the Information Technology Council acts as a mini Board of Directors. Its job is to provide guidance to ensure that the partnership stays within the guidelines and intent as established in the initial contract. As the partnership evolves, the Information Technology Council will prove to be a means of ensuring that both companies are achieving the goals and objectives originally set forth, but also of identifying and actively pursuing new ways of improving the partnership.

The only way an outsourcing agreement will stand the test of time is to ensure that you have developed a very positive business partnership with the outsourcing firm. As everyone knows, it is easy to have companies that you do business with on a supplier and customer basis. The length of time involved, combined with the large scope and amount of money involved, dictates that the outsourcing agreement must go far beyond the supplier and customer relationship.

A true partnership must be developed to ensure that both companies receive the benefits and rewards that a partnership can bring. Forming this partnership is an essential part of the overall outsourcing process. Since you will be with the outsourcing firm for an extended period of time, it is essential that both parties understand and truly believe that the partnership exists. If necessary, the outsourcing process should be prolonged to ensure that all the necessary elements are in place that will give the partnership a fair chance of survival.

When you start to think about how to build a partnership, you should identify the primary characteristics that would be important for your company and its business partners. The characteristics will change from company to company, depending upon many variables. A few of the characteristics that one might consider are:

1. Corporate culture
2. Company reputation
3. Market position
4. Core competencies
5. Primary weaknesses
6. Financial stability
7. Experience in your industry
8. The chemistry between the outsourcing firm's Account Manager and your company
9. Identifying the benefits for both companies

This list of characteristics comprises the majority of the things that most companies look for in a partnership. To better illustrate the importance of each characteristic, let's take a closer look at each one in detail.

Corporate Culture

Given the lengthy nature of outsourcing partnerships, it is highly advisable to ensure that your company and the outsourcing company's basic business philosophies are complementary. This is not to say that the two companies have to be identical in their thinking and strategic goals. It does, however, imply that the two companies should share in their vision of what makes a company and partnership successful.

Company Reputation

An important factor to consider when determining who you would like to have for your business partner is the potential business partner's reputation in the industry. The last thing you would want is to associate your company's name with another company that has a reputation of being less than outstanding in its field of expertise.

Information Systems outsourcing, as a whole, has been around for many years, but it has not been until recently that outsourcing has become a viable solution for many companies. In this day of corporate downsizing and focusing on core competencies, Information Systems outsourcing has become a very popular strategic move. To respond to this market demand, many outsourcing firms have evolved from other Information Systems services-related companies. For example, a few companies offering outsourcing services today were strictly computer-related hardware sales and distribution companies a couple of years ago. As computer hardware sales margins continued to erode, combined with fierce competition, these companies decided to branch off into the highly profitable business of Information Systems outsourcing.

It is easy to see that the Information Systems outsourcing industry is fairly new and surprisingly small. This makes it fairly simple to find out what the reputation for any given outsourcing firm is in the marketplace. Due to the relatively small number of companies that offer outsourcing services, it is highly likely that everyone in the business knows of each other.

Selecting an outsourcing firm that has less than a stellar reputation will make it more difficult for the partnership to succeed and significantly toughen your job of getting your recommendation approved by your Board of Directors. You may be convinced that the outsourcing firm that you are thinking about partnering with is the best selection for your company, but if their reputation is not what it should be, then your risk of success is greatly increased. This is not to say that you cannot be successful in this type of partnership, but it would certainly take more effort for both your company and the outsourcing firm to overcome the obvious obstacles that would be prevalent in the beginning of the partnership.

Market Position

Market position is a characteristic that will help to assess the viability of partnering with a given outsourcing firm. If the outsourcing firm's market position dominates the market, then it is highly likely the initial advertising that is associated with outsourcing may not be as widespread as with an outsourcing firm that is looking to increase its market share. Partnering with an outsourcing firm that is striving to increase market share can also be beneficial.

Since your company would be a newly formed partnership for the outsourcing firm, your account may have a higher level of visibility than long-term existing accounts with the same outsourcing firm. As a result, the outsourcing firm's prospects will most likely want to speak with representatives from your company to perform their own reference check. As such, the outsourcing firm will be doing everything in its power to ensure that you and everybody else in your company is satisfied with the newly formed partnership.

This by no means implies that the larger outsourcing firms which hold the majority of the market share would not also be responsive to the needs of your company. After all, the larger outsourcing firms did not get where they are by ignoring their customer base. Therefore, it is safe to assume that the larger outsourcing firms will do everything possible and feasible to ensure a successful partnership.

When considering a business partner, market share can be used to identify the outsourcing firm's position in the industry. Comparing market share over a period of time can also be a good indication of how aggressive and competitive your potential business partner will be.

Core Competencies

When we think about outsourcing Information Systems, it is generally thought that the outsourcing firms can provide any Information Systems-related service that you may require. However, this is not the case. Many Information Systems outsourcing firms specialize in specific areas. For example, one company may specialize in application services, while another specializes in networking services. Telecommunications, application services, hardware services, desktop services, networking services, administrative applications, help desk, and many more are all services in which outsourcing companies may specialize. There are also outsourcing firms that specialize in multiple disciplines, but not all. When considering who you would like to have for your business partner, I always like to think that I would select a service provider that can provide any Information Systems services that I may need today or potentially need in the future.

There certainly isn't anything wrong with selecting an outsourcing firm that specializes in something less than the entire Information Systems discipline. However, it is important to ensure that you understand what these limitations are and what the core competency is for the business partner you are considering. If the outsourcing firm is pursuing additional market share, there will be a point in time at which the outsourcing firm will have to offer more than they currently have in terms of core competencies. Therefore, it is feasible to think that there are many outsourcing firms that today may specialize in specific areas but will offer full Information Systems services in the future. If you want to partner with one of these firms, be certain you understand its core competencies and its plan for increasing its service offering in the future.

Primary Weaknesses

There is an old saying that everyone has weaknesses. This can also be said for companies. Regardless of a company's competitive position, market share, or service offerings, each outsourcing firm will have its areas of weakness. While most company representatives will be forthcoming and, when asked, will tell you specifically where their areas of weakness are, not all company representatives will be as direct as you would like. As a result, it is up to you and your Outsourcing Team to define the outsourcing firm's weaknesses and compare them to your company's weaknesses. Again, all companies have weakness.

In a true partnership, the two companies should complement each other by one providing strengths where the other one is weak. Once the Outsourcing Team has a good understanding of where the weaknesses lie for both companies, a comparison can be made. If you find that both your company and the outsourcing firm share a common weakness, this is an area that should be highlighted as a potential risk factor for the success of the partnership. In this event, it would be advisable to include this common weakness in your risk assessment as discussed in Chapter 5, "Proposal Evaluations."

Financial Stability

When entering into a partnership, it is common to consider the financial stability of both partners. If an outsourcing firm is a financially strong company, then this would not be an area of concern. However, if the financial history and current status of an outsourcing firm has less than a superior rating, you may want to question the viability of the partnership. When outsourcing, there is enough risk involved in managing the unknown events that will definitely occur during the life of the agreement. As such, you may want to question the feasibility of partnering with an outsourcing firm that may be in financial trouble or is not as financially strong as you would like.

You and your Outsourcing Team will have enough risks and issues to worry about without knowingly adding a risk such as the financial problems of an outsourcing firm. Assuming the outsourcing firm is a publicly held company, it is very easy to obtain the financial history that you will need to make this assessment. In the event the outsourcing firm is privately held, you will have a much more difficult time obtaining the financial data necessary to make an informed decision. One method for obtaining this information for a privately held outsourcing firm is to include this topic in the line of questions that you have when checking the outsourcing firm's references.

The bottom line on financial stability is: if the outsourcing firm is having financial difficulties, it is highly advisable to select another outsourcing firm as your business partner.

Experience in Your Industry

The positive characteristic to consider in a business partner is the amount of experience that an Information Systems outsourcing firm has in your specific industry. Since Information Systems are provided across all companies within all industries, it is common to find an outsourcing firm that provides services for many different industries. While there are many similarities in Information Systems regardless of the industry, there are industry-specific requirements that the Information Systems discipline must meet. For example, the banking industry and the manufacturing industry are two totally different types of environment. Both share the common function of Information Systems, but Information Systems in each industry is significantly different. As a result, it is highly advisable to select a partner that has an in-depth understanding of your specific industry. Doing so will increase the likelihood of a successful and long-lasting partnership.

Selecting a business partner that has little or no experience in your industry does not mean that the partnership cannot succeed. However, it does mean that you will have to pay closer attention to the fact that the outsourcing firm does not have experience in your specific area of expertise.

The Chemistry Between the Outsourcing Firm's Account Manager and Your Company

It is advisable to insist that the outsourcing firm include the potential Account Manager in the pre-sales discussions in contract negotiations. Doing so will increase your comfort level with the individual who will have sole responsibility within the outsourcing firm for seeing that the partnership between your company and the outsourcing firm is a success. If for whatever reason you find that the Account Manager is not suited for your company, you should immediately notify the outsourcing firm's next level of management.

There are so many things that can damage a business partnership that when a potential obstacle is identified, it should be immediately researched and resolved. The outsourcing firm's Account Manager will be the absolute key to the success of the partnership. It is essential that the individual fit within your organization. Electing to overlook an issue in this area would be a grave mistake and could potentially negate any chance for the partnership to succeed. As a result, it is only fair to your company, the outsourcing firm, and the Account Manager to identify this issue in the event it should occur.

Identifying the Benefits for Both Companies

A partnership can only succeed when all partners benefit as a result of the partnership. With this in mind, it is advisable to have a list that specifically identifies the benefits for your company as well as your potential business partner. If you find that the list is significantly one-sided, you may want to reevaluate your decision as to which outsourcing firm you would like as a partner.

It is natural to think that the benefits would be primarily on your company's side of the comparison. After all, this is why you are outsourcing to begin with — to achieve the benefits that are typically associated with outsourcing. Benefits such as reduced costs, reduced risks, increased technology, a strengthened competitive position for your company, etc., are all benefits that your company should expect as a result of outsourcing. Commonly overlooked are the benefits accruing to the outsourcing firm in partnering with your company. Examples of the outsourcing firm's potential benefits would be:

- Increasing market share
- Increasing competitive position
- Aligning themselves with a leader in a specific industry
- Improving profit
- Establishing a presence in the country, state, or region

When comparing the benefits for both your company and the outsourcing firm, you should find that both companies stand to benefit equally as a result of partnering with each other. If this is not the case, I would suggest reconsidering the overall scope of the outsourcing agreement and the company you have selected as a business partner.

The above list examines a few of the characteristics you may want to consider when establishing a business partnership. I am sure there will be additional characteristics for your specific company that are not included here. Regardless of what the characteristics are, this step is an important one and should not be omitted during the outsourcing process. This procedure can also be used to assist you in the early outsourcing process to determine if you are working with the correct outsourcing firms. Since this part of the process should be done early in the overall outsourcing initiative, it can also save you from wasting time with a potential business partner that does not fit your overall business acumen.

After considering the characteristics that you have identified and finding that the potential outsourcing partner has scored positively in each of the categories, it is often asked, "How do you know if this is still the right partner to select?" There are no certain answers for this question. As long as you and your Outsourcing Team have done a thorough job of identifying your requirements and assessing the strengths and weaknesses of the outsourcing firm, and the outsourcing firm scores well in all the categories, it often comes down to a "leap of faith" that you must take. As long as you have done your job well, used consulting assistance where needed, and have taken an open-minded approach in your assessment, there is no reason to think that the business partner you select would be anything less than the right one.

There is an old saying that "it takes years to build a partnership and a few seconds to lose one." This is appropriate and true when entering into an outsourcing partnership. Care should be taken throughout the entire process of selecting an outsourcing firm as well as the long-term management of the partnership. Never take anything for granted, always follow through on assigned tasks, and always keep the lines of communication open with your outsourcing firm. Building a partnership is one of the most difficult, and one of the most rewarding, things to achieve in business. It takes a lot of hard work on your part as well as the outsourcing firm's to achieve and maintain this goal.

4 | Request For Proposals

To adequately price a contract, the outsourcing firm must have a clear understanding of the scope of the work to be done. Without this definition, there is a strong possibility that the outsourcing firm and/or your company will not include critical tasks that the outsourcing firm will be expected to complete. The best way to identify these tasks, and provide enough information to the outsourcing firm, is to develop a request for proposal (RFP). A request for proposal is a document that should describe:

- Your company
- Your specific processing environment
- Your business concerns
- Strategic directions
- The benefits you are hoping to achieve in an outsourcing agreement
- Current and future forecasted costs
- Company background
- Company products
- Your market position and description
- Specific directions on the bidding process

The above is a partial list of topics that should be included in the request for proposal. These and many other facts are necessary to support the outsourcing decision. To say the least, writing a request for proposal is not a trivial task. A great deal of time and effort should be devoted to developing a specific request for proposal that clearly defines your requirements and the success factors that will determine if outsourcing is right for your company. The request for proposal will also be the document that will assist you in determining which outsourcer is right for your specific needs.

If you elect to sole-source (select one outsourcing firm to deal with and not compete the business) the outsourcing business, you will still need to know the information that is generated during a typical request for proposal effort. Sole-sourcing is risky. It eliminates all competition for the selected outsourcing firm. Depending on the outsourcing firm, this may remove any desire on their part to negotiate competitively. Once selected as a sole-source provider, the outsourcing firm's only competitor will be your internal Information Systems organization. All they have to do is beat the price and/or add value over the internal Information Systems organization to win the business. There is a place for sole-sourcing, but be certain it is being done for the right reasons. Be sure you are comfortable with the capabilities of the outsourcing firm you have selected and ensure the proper checks and balances are used throughout the outsourcing process. Regardless of whether or not you put the business up for competitive bid, you should generate the request for proposal. Do not underestimate the importance of data generated during the request for proposal effort. You will need the information to communicate with the outsourcing firm and for generation of the Statement of Work and the contract.

While it is possible to have outside assistance in writing the request for proposal, the majority of the work must be done by internal personnel. Only those individuals with a complete understanding of your business and specific needs should participate in the development of the request for proposal. The most effective way to write the request for proposal is to assign the appropriate sections of the document to the various members of the outsourcing committee. Typically, the outsourcing committee chairman will either coordinate the development of the document or assign the responsibility to another member of the team.

You will gather information during the outsourcing strategy activities (as discussed in Chapter 2, "Developing An Outsourcing Strategy") that will be useful in writing the request for proposal. But this alone is not enough. you will need many more details about the specifics of your business and your requirements. During this phase of the process you will begin to realize the amount of information that is going to be required to adequately define what the outsourcers will need. This should not be a deterrent but rather a time to reconfirm your company's commitment to proceed with outsourcing. This is also not the time to take shortcuts. A well-thought-out and well-structured request for proposal will take a great deal of time to develop. However, your investment in time to produce the request for proposal will be rewarded.

Generally speaking, for every hour you spend on developing a request for proposal, you will save at least two hours later in the process.

Many companies will utilize the "war room" concept for developing a request for proposal. In this environment, each member of the Outsourcing Team will be assigned an area on the walls in the war room. Each team member should be responsible for developing a specific section of the request for proposal. The latest version of their section should be posted on the appropriate wall area that was assigned to them. Where feasible, illustrations should be used to highlight concerns and help explain the requirement or current environment. As the request for proposal evolves, there should be a minimum of two, and optimally three, reviews by a "red team."

The red team should consist of members from senior management whose responsibility will be to review the entire request for proposal and suggest appropriate changes. Scheduling these reviews throughout the request for proposal development process will help to ensure a quality document and minimize the risk of omitting crucial information. Once the Outsourcing Team feels comfortable that the document is ready to be released, there should be one last red team review. During this review, final comments and corrections are made with the Outsourcing Team members, and the final decision as to when the request for proposal should be released will be made.

During this process you will find just how well you have documented your business processes. Many times a company realizes that its processes are not adequately documented, and the request for proposal is placed on hold until this documentation is developed. Again, the whole outsourcing process is a time when your total Information Systems organization is reviewed in detail and provides an excellent opportunity to clean house as you go through the process. While it may be a laborious and painstaking task, this information is vital to the outsourcers. This is the only means they have of determining the size and scope of the task on which they will be bidding. Typical areas that are usually not fully documented are:

- Service levels
- Software and hardware licenses
- Software and hardware maintenance agreements
- Assets (e.g., personal computers, printers, etc.)
- Location and ownership identification
- Internal Information Technology standards

One would think that any Information Systems organization would have good control and documentation for their software and hardware licenses and maintenance agreements with their suppliers. However, once this information is reviewed, it usually is found to be incomplete. Obviously, if you are going to be asking the outsourcing firm to assume responsibility for your hardware and software, you will have to have current documentation and a clear understanding of exactly what your contractual obligations are with each supplier.

In order to adequately define the systems performance standards, you must have your service levels defined. The service levels should address the hardware and physical layer of your computing architecture. Also included in the service level documentation would be the personnel-related service levels. Some examples are:

- Companies with a help desk generally have a "Call Close Rate" (a percentage of problems that are resolved during the initial call).
- Application development professionals may have a performance measure that tracks the number of days it takes to correct a software maintenance-related problem.
- Telecommunications personnel may have performance measures established for the length of time it takes to do telephone installations, moves, and changes.
- Systems operations generally track performance measures such as the percentage of time the central processing unit (CPU) is active and the availability rate of mission-critical components (e.g., the mainframe, network file servers, etc.).

These services will certainly vary from company to company but, in general, the concept is to identify what you expect the outsourcing firm to accomplish. Illustrated in Figure 4.1 is a typical management report for tracking service level performance. This type of document can be used to report the actual performance compared to the standards established in the contract. Also included is a sample Service Level Agreement, contained in Appendix B. These documents should be used as guidelines for establishing your actual service levels. While the actual service level documents will vary, the basic objective is to document the performance that you expect from your internal Information Systems organization today as compared to what you would expect to achieve from an outsourcing firm.

INFORMATION SYSTEMS MONTHLY PERFORMANCE REPORT

	Goal	Previous Month	Current Month	6 Month Average
System Availability (percent)				
Voice	99.999	100	99.955	99.998
Mainframe	99.999	98.565	100	99.000
Network	99.999	99.025	100	98.995
Response Time (seconds)				
Mainframe	0.8	0.9	0.9	0.9
Network	1.0	1.0	1.1	1.0
Call Close Rate (percent)	60	58	61	62
Lines of Code per Programmer	30	32	25	28
Number of User Devices With Downtime Occurrences	20	18	24	22
Cost as a Percent of Sales	1.2	1.3	1.4	1.4
Number of Job Reruns	0	0	2	1
Number of Reports Distributed Behind Schedule	0	2	5	3

Figure 4.1　Service Level Performance Report

Non-data center assets (e.g., personal computers) seem to be an issue for all Chief Information Officers. We all know it is impossible for personal computers to be relocated without assistance, but there are many Chief Information Officers who will swear they "move themselves" from one desk to another. The personal computer has become such a common fixture in offices that employees think of them no differently than they would a typewriter in the 1950s. If it is needed elsewhere in the building, employees move it there. While they do exist, it is rare to find a company that has a reliable tracking system for desktop devices.

This dilemma is caused by many factors, the least of which is the portability of the equipment. This is compounded by the fact that for every new personal computer purchased, there is an average of three additional personal computers to be relocated somewhere in the organization. I call this the "hand-me-down" syndrome. For example, Joe will buy a new personal computer and give his old personal computer to Harry. Then Harry will give his old personal computer to Mary, and so on, until all traceability of where your PCs are located is lost unless there is a rock-solid tracking method in place to avoid this dilemma. So, if you are expecting the outsourcing firm to take responsibility for the physical ownership and/or the maintenance of these personal computers and peripherals, you must be able to identify the total number of personal computers and their locations.

Everyone understands the benefits of having good internal Information Systems standards. But it is amazing to see the number of companies that have not kept their internal standards current. They rely on the more experienced long-term employees to teach newer employees about the development and service standards for the Information Systems organization. Again, if you expect the outsourcing firm to adhere to your standards, then the standards must be well documented. The employees who transition as part of the initial outsourcing agreement may not be the same employees working on your account in the future. Therefore, you must have good documentation to be able to pass along the standards from one individual to another.

At a minimum, the request for proposal should contain four sections:

1. General information *for* the bidders
2. Company background information
3. General requirements
4. Information required *from* the bidders

Provided in Appendix C is a suggested table of contents for an outsourcing request for proposal. As you can see, each of the four sections above is identified in the outline with the appropriate subsections. This sample request for proposal outline is provided as a guideline only; the actual request for proposal must be tailored to your specific requirements and overall organization. The illustrated table of contents is intended to provoke thought and ideas with regard to how an outsourcing request for proposal should be structured.

EVENT	DATE
Release Date Of RFP	June 2, 1997
Last Date For Accepting Questions	July 1, 1997
Proposal Due	July 15, 1997
Oral Presentations	September 18-19, 1997
Select Final 2-3 Bidders	November 18, 1997
Notification Of Contract Award	January 6, 1998

Figure 4.2   Proposal Schedule

The first section of the request for proposal should deal with the general information for the bidders about the specific request for proposal and the proposal process. This section should include all information that would be necessary for a bidder to respond to the request for proposal. The purpose of the request for proposal should be clearly stated with enough detail to define the high-level scope of the contract. A schedule should also be provided which depicts the anticipated dates for major events in your specific out-sourcing process. Figure 4.2 contains an example of a proposal schedule.

By this time, you should now have a good understanding of the various tasks that must be completed during the outsourcing process. It would be appropriate to develop a project plan and include a copy of the plan in the request for proposal. Again, this should be included in the first section of the request for proposal to give the bidders the opportunity to see the tasks that you feel are important. I would highly recommend developing the project plan with a personal computer-based project management software package. There are many packages on the market that provide the capabilities that would be required. A good project plan will contain the major steps that must occur, the scheduled start and stop dates, and the names of the persons responsible for completing the tasks. Having this information in a project management software package gives you the flexibility of changing, adding, and deleting tasks as necessary and seeing the immediate impact on the overall project. Figure 4.3 on the following 6 pages contains a sample out-sourcing project plan for your review.

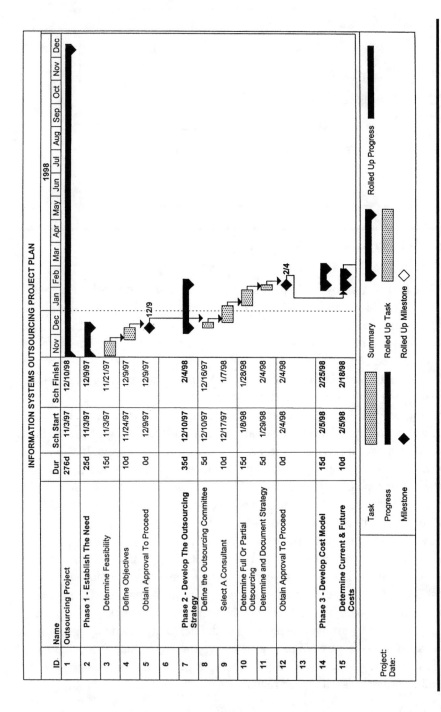

Figure 4.3   Sample Outsourcing Project Plan

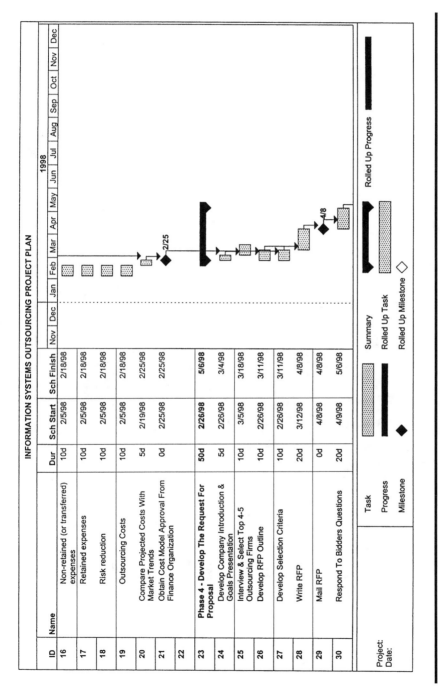

Figure 4.3   Sample Outsourcing Project Plan (continued)

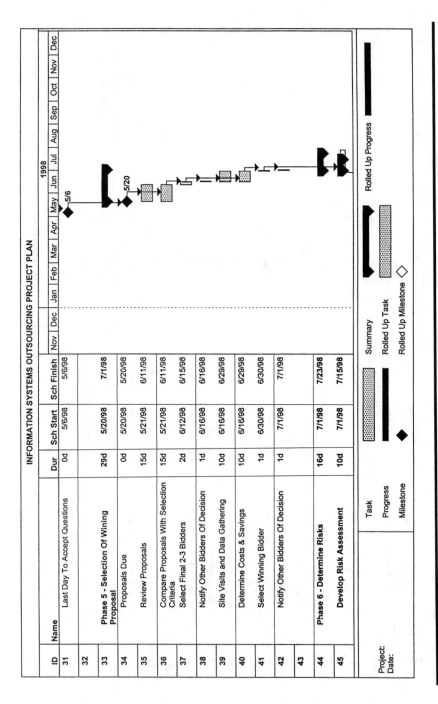

Figure 4.3   Sample Outsourcing Project Plan (continued)

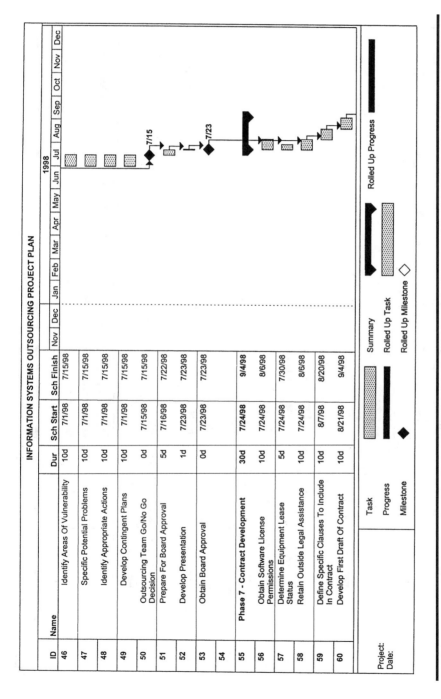

Figure 4.3   Sample Outsourcing Project Plan (continued)

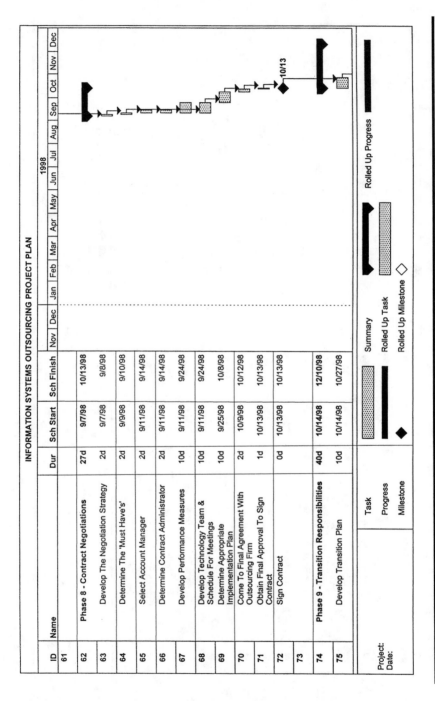

INFORMATION SYSTEMS OUTSOURCING PROJECT PLAN

ID	Name	Dur	Sch Start	Sch Finish
61				
62	Phase 8 - Contract Negotiations	27d	9/7/98	10/13/98
63	Develop The Negotiation Strategy	2d	9/7/98	9/8/98
64	Determine The 'Must Have's'	2d	9/9/98	9/10/98
65	Select Account Manager	2d	9/11/98	9/14/98
66	Determine Contract Administrator	2d	9/11/98	9/14/98
67	Develop Performance Measures	10d	9/11/98	9/24/98
68	Develop Technology Team & Schedule For Meetings	10d	9/11/98	9/24/98
69	Determine Appropriate Implementation Plan	10d	9/25/98	10/8/98
70	Come To Final Agreement With Outsourcing Firm	2d	10/9/98	10/12/98
71	Obtain Final Approval To Sign Contract	1d	10/13/98	10/13/98
72	Sign Contract	0d	10/13/98	10/13/98
73				
74	Phase 9 - Transition Responsibilities	40d	10/14/98	12/10/98
75	Develop Transition Plan	10d	10/14/98	10/27/98

Task Progress Milestone Summary Rolled Up Task Rolled Up Milestone Rolled Up Progress

Project:
Date:

Figure 4.3 Sample Outsourcing Project Plan (continued)

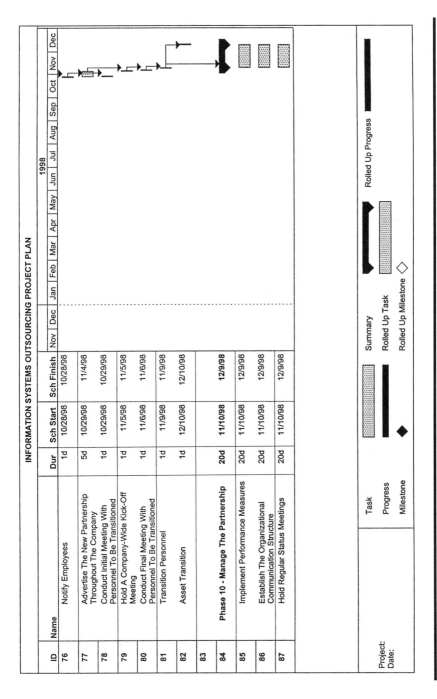

Figure 4.3   Sample Outsourcing Project Plan (continued)

As illustrated in Appendix C, there are many other topics to be addressed in the first section of the request for proposal. The most important topics address how the bidder's proposal must be structured, the selection criteria, how the contract will be awarded, and the contract payment schedule. This information will specifically inform the bidders as to what you will be looking for in their proposals and the actual criteria by which you will be measuring their specific ability to meet your requirements. It is also important to state that, while the proposal will have a significant impact on the final decision, the final decision will be based upon additional criteria as well. One such criterion is the information learned during site visits to a few of the outsourcing firm's existing customers. During these visits you will have the opportunity to speak with personnel who have already been through the outsourcing process. The results of these visits will be valuable in assessing the overall impact of outsourcing and the management style of the outsourcing firm.

The request for proposal should be explicit in specifying the selection criteria. This section should be expanded to include the details necessary to give the bidders a thorough understanding of how you will be determining the contract winner. Further, the selection criteria section describes the evaluation process used to determine which proposal maximizes the benefits to your company in relation to cost, security, competence, experience, timely performance, maintenance, and all other stated objectives. A thoroughly written selection criteria section of the request for proposal will contain, at a minimum, the following topics:

A. General — A brief description of how the proposal evaluation process will proceed.
B. Primary Objectives — A description of the primary objectives of the evaluation process.
C. Evaluation Process Description — A description of each phase of the evaluation process.
D. Evaluation Phases
    1. Examine proposals for compliance with request for proposal instructions.
    2. Evaluate and score proposals — Points are based on the following criteria:
       a. Capability and qualifications
       b. Technical approach
       c. Qualified personnel

d. Price
3. Determine proposal compliance with pass/fail requirements — A review to determine if the proposal meets the minimum standards. The suggested minimum standards are:
   a. Outsourcing agreements with others
   b. Operating environment
   c. Provisions for new development and growth
   d. Guaranteed support and staffing levels
   e. Technical and technology advantage
   f. Transition
4. Prepare evaluation report and recommendation.
5. Determine apparent successful bidder.

The second section of the request for proposal deals strictly with information about your company background and overall organizational structure. Information provided in this section should give enough detail for the bidders to understand the type of business you are in and the history of the systems environment that led to the decision to consider outsourcing as a viable alternative. However, the discussion should not be focused solely upon systems. Outsourcing today means forming a partnership that will provide benefits across your organization, and not just be limited to your Information Systems organization. Great care should be taken throughout the request for proposal to ensure that no proprietary information is disclosed. This is a document that will most likely be mailed to multiple outsourcing companies. You cannot control the distribution of the documents after you have mailed them. It is advisable to use caution when writing the request for proposal to ensure that the information being provided is accurate and detailed enough for the bidders to provide their assessment but not divulge information you do not wish your competitors to obtain.

The third section should contain your specific requirements. It should also contain your overall corporate scope and objectives for the outsourcing activity. For larger companies that have multiple plants and sites, a section should be devoted to each specific location. Your requirements and specifications should be given in detail so that the bidders fully understand what your requirements are and have a good appreciation of the scope of the outsourcing agreement. This specification should include a detailed description of the Information Systems organization and all the responsibilities required of the outsourcer. Some examples of the specifications that should be included in this section are:

- Information Systems Organization — A description of the Information Systems organization and how it is currently structured. This organization description should include each position of the organization, whether or not it is considered part of the outsourcing agreement. The description of each position should include:
  - The basic job description
  - Technical and professional qualifications
  - Education requirements
  - Business objects for the position
- Application Software Description — A detailed description of all application software being utilized. Regardless of the type of software, the description should include the basic purpose for the software and its amount of usage (in terms of number of users). Application software should include all business applications (except administrative software, e.g., word processing, spreadsheet, and graphic generation software, etc.) regardless of the hardware platform in which it resides. This description should include each module of the software (e.g., material control, accounts payable, etc.) and whether the software is custom developed or from a third-party supplier. In the event of third-party software, there should be a detailed description of the extent to which the software has been modified.
- User Environment — Identify the number of users of the systems and the general level of user effectiveness in utilizing the application software. Additional facts such as centralized versus decentralized applications, average amount of experience using the software, etc., would be helpful for the outsourcing firm to know.
- The Computing Environment — Provide a detailed description of the mainframe and/or mid-range computers and their peripherals. Included would be:
  - The amount of direct access storage devices (DASD) storage available
  - DASD current utilization rate
  - The throughput (measured in transactions per hour)
  - CPU utilization rate
  - Amount of memory
  - Tape drives (including model and type)
  - Disk drives (including model and type)
  - Other storage media (including model and type)
  - Controllers

- Terminals
- Communications adapters
- Uninterruptable power supply (UPS)

Also included in this section would be the operating system software and the system-related software such as, compilers, databases, file transfer, query, reporting writers, etc.

- Networking — This section should contain a detailed description of the local area network (LAN) architecture including hardware components, software (both system and administrative support), and the overall topology of the network. The topology description should include a diagram of the LAN, the number of file servers, print servers, routers, bridges, gateways, printers, type of cabling (e.g., coax, fiber optics, twisted pair, etc.), and hubs. Also included in this section should be a description of your wide area network (WAN) if applicable. The WAN description should contain the same level of detail as described in the LAN description and should include a diagram of all physical locations on the WAN, and the configuration for each location.
- Internet — This section should include a detailed description of your company's use of the Internet. All web sites should also be specified. Information such as identification of your Internet provider, frequency of updates, third-party development companies being utilized to maintain the existing sites, etc., should be provided.
- Hardware and Software Maintenance — A detailed description should be provided that clearly defines how you are currently maintaining all hardware and software. In the case of LAN, personal computer, and related peripherals, you should specifically show how this equipment is being diagnosed and repaired in your environment today. A clear description of maintenance agreements that you currently have with outside suppliers, such as mainframe maintenance and application maintenance agreements with software suppliers, should also be included in this section.
- Training — Include a detailed description of how you are currently providing end-user training and technical training for the Information Systems staff. The frequency of the training should also be included. Ongoing (internal and external) training for Information Systems personnel should also be included in this section.

- Help Desk — If you are currently utilizing a help desk, you should describe how the help desk is being utilized from a staffing position and the end-user interface position. Also included in this section should be the frequency of calls, the average number of calls you have in an "open" status, the average number of calls received daily, and the average number of calls that are "closed" daily. Lastly, include how you handle the help desk calls received during non-prime time hours (for example, 24 hours a day, seven days a week operations in a manufacturing plant).

- Inventories — A detailed inventory list should be provided which identifies all equipment and its location. Also included in this section should be a detailed list of all software (system and application).

- Security — Information should be provided describing the current level of security required throughout the processing environment. Included in this description should be the security information for the mainframe, LAN, WAN, and Internet access.

- Operational Support — A description of how computer operations are maintained on a 24-hour, 7-day basis should be provided. Also included should be a description of how off-hour support is maintained in the area of applications.

- Telecommunications — This section should provide: a detailed description of the type, model, and size of your private branch exchange (PBXs); the number of telephonic devices supported; the configuration of the PBX; voice mail system configuration; and automated call distribution (ACD) configuration and utilization. If multiple sites are involved, a diagram of the telecommunications network would be appropriate, as well as a list of the local and long distance carriers being utilized (and if appropriate, your telecommunications aggregator).

- Growth — The request for proposal should contain your estimate of what your growth projections are, from a system and user standpoint, for the foreseeable future. In the event no growth is anticipated or a downsizing activity is imminent, then this should also be stated.

- Contracts — A listing should be provided of all current contracts with hardware and software suppliers; service providers (include the name of the company); the name of the products on contract; renewal date; and in the case of software, the current version installed.

■ Leases — This section should contain a description of the current leases (operating and capital). The list should contain the leasing company name, point of contact, address, telephone number, and the lease termination date.

The fourth and final section of the request for proposal should contain specific information that you require from the suppliers. This section should be specific in identifying the format of the proposal and ensure that you have a means of comparing one bidder's proposal with another. As you will find in the next chapter, "Proposal Evaluations," there will be specific guidelines to determine if bidders are meeting your requirements. Enforcing the structure of the bidder's proposals to a specific format will make this task much easier and eliminate the need to spend time searching through multiple documents to obtain the answers you need.

Going through the request for proposal process is important to ensure the bidders have a thorough understanding of the tasks required and the scope of the total project. It is also a means for you to determine how well the bidders understand your specific situations and needs. Take the time to ensure the request for proposal provides enough detail to adequately describe the reasons you feel outsourcing is a viable option and the specific benefits you feel will be achieved as a result of outsourcing. Remember, the more research you do at the outset and the more thorough the request for proposal, the less time will be required later in the outsourcing process. For example, if a topic is not covered adequately in the request for proposal, you will have to answer the questions and address the topic with each of the bidders individually instead of just once in the request for proposal. While it is impossible to include every single detail of your daily activities in a request for proposal, great care should be taken to ensure that most of the work is done at this point rather than waiting until later when the time required will be magnified several times.

Lastly, the request for proposal should follow the theme of your stated outsourcing strategy. This theme should be carried through the entire outsourcing process, as everything must relate to the strategy. That is not to say that the strategy cannot be refined during the outsourcing process, but everything must relate to the strategy because it will be the guideline that will ensure that all requirements and expectations are met.

5 | Proposal Evaluations

After receiving proposals from the prospective outsourcing firms, you will most likely start to realize that, after a cursory review, all bidders seem to meet your stated requirements. At that point, you may start to be concerned about having gone through all the work of writing a request for proposal only to realize that all bidders are meeting your requirements and seem to be equally qualified. This concern will be short lived once you start the detailed evaluation of each proposal. The process for proposal evaluation should be well thought out and documented. As you were developing the request for proposal, one of the sections should have been "Selection Criteria." The selection criteria in the request for proposal explains to the bidders the process you are going to use to evaluate their ability to meet your requirements. For the bidders, the selection criteria are nothing more than an overview of the details you should have developed for evaluating the proposals.

It is important to remember that the result of the proposal evaluation will be the recommendation or selection of one outsourcing firm to focus on during the next several months of the outsourcing process. As a result, it is extremely important that you pay attention to detail and do not take shortcuts during the proposal evaluation process. The evaluation should be a team effort, consisting of the Outsourcing Team as well as any additional assistance required from both inside and outside your company. For example, if the proposal consists of implementing new technologies that are not currently utilized, you may want to obtain an opinion from an industry expert to comment on the proposed technical solution.

While there are many techniques used in the proposal evaluations, there are five primary methods that seem to work best. The methods are:

1. Go/No Go decision analysis
2. Weighted decision analysis
3. Cost and benefit analysis
4. Risk assessment
5. Confidence assessment

The following sections describe each of the five methods and how to apply them during your proposal evaluation process.

Go/No Go Decision Analysis

What must the outsourcer do? What would the team like them to do? What constraints affect the choice of an outsourcer? Such are the questions the Outsourcing Team must ask in order to begin setting priorities and defining the absolute requirements for finding a successful outsourcing firm. The answers to these questions will result in a list of objectives. The objectives should then be classified as "must haves" or "desirables."

Each "must have" is considered mandatory and should be measurable. An outsourcer might offer each feature or it might not. The list of desirable objectives represents additional but not mandatory criteria. In an evaluation, alternatives either meet all the "must have" objectives (creating a "Go" condition) or they do not (creating a "No Go" condition). An outsourcer that scores one or more No Go rating is immediately dropped from further consideration. Figure 5.1 represents a sample of a Go/No Go Analysis. The actual Go/No Go criteria will vary from company to company. Utilizing this type of analysis allows you to quickly identify those companies that cannot meet your minimum requirements. This prevents you from spending valuable time on outsourcing firms that would eventually be eliminated from the list of alternatives.

The list of "must haves" should be carefully defined. The goal is to generate the absolute requirements that an outsourcing firm must meet. If your team decides to use the method in the evaluation phase, the Outsourcing Team must be ready to disqualify a bidder in the event the bidder cannot provide any of the "must haves." The "must haves" and the overall Go/No Go strategy should be carefully communicated to the bidders. This will assist you in explaining why a bidder was eliminated from further consideration in the event one or more bidders failed to meet all of the "must have" requirements.

#	Requirement	Company				
		A	B	C	D	E
1	Does the supplier have a global presence?	GO	GO	GO	GO	NO GO
2	Does the supplier offer a full range of IT services?	GO	GO	GO	GO	GO
3	Does the supplier have an existing customer base of companies that are similar?	GO	GO	GO	GO	GO
4	Is the supplier experienced in business process re-engineering?	GO	GO	GO	NO GO	GO
5	Is the supplier price competitive?	GO	GO	GO	GO	NO GO
6	Does the supplier have experience working with your application software?	GO	GO	GO	GO	NO GO

Figure 5.1   Sample Go/No Go Decision Analysis

Weighted Decision Analysis

The purpose of the Weighted Decision analysis is to assist the Outsourcing Team in distinguishing which objectives are more important than others. Without the Weighted Decision analysis, all requirements carry equal weight. This could potentially be a disastrous result for your company. For example, if you don't distinguish the importance of one requirement from another, the requirement for an outsourcing firm to provide onsite technical support would carry the same importance as a lessor requirement, such as providing janitorial services for the computer room. As a result, it is essential that you use some sort of a Weighted Decision analysis.

After the outsourcing firms pass the Go/No Go analysis, their abilities to meet the desirable objectives are measured via the Weighted Decision analysis. Once the desirable objectives have been identified, each one should be weighted according to its relative importance. The most important objective is identified and given a weight of 10. All others are then weighted in comparison with the first, from 10 (highly important) down to a possible 1 (not very important).

No attempt is made to rank the objectives. The purpose of the 10–1 weighting scale is simply to make visible the relationships among these objectives. What matters most? What could be done without, if necessary? When the time comes to evaluate the alternatives, you would do so by assessing them relative to each other against all desirable objectives — one at a time. This is why it is critical at the outset to identify the most important objectives. It is pointless to know that a particular alternative satisfies 9 out of 10 desirable objectives if, in fact, it is the 10th that is the most crucial to the success of the decision. You should also examine the balance of desirable objectives and look for certain danger signals:

- Too many high numbers may indicate either unrealistic expectations or a faulty perception of which objectives can guarantee success.
- Too many low numbers suggest that unimportant details may be "smothering" the analysis.
- Too many objectives reflecting the vested interest of a single department may lead to an unworkable decision. This is especially true if other departments are equally affected by the final decision.
- Loaded objectives — those that guarantee a smooth passage for a certain alternative and blackball all others — can make a mockery of an analysis.

The results of the weighted decision analysis will identify weak areas that must be shored up during the contract negotiating process. Figure 5.2 illustrates a typical weighted decision analysis. As you can see, the analysis is particularly helpful in identifying the one or two outsourcing firms that appear to be bubbling to the top of the list as viable candidates. When done properly, the bidder with the highest score best fits your overall objectives.

Cost And Benefit Analysis

The cost and benefit analysis provides a means to assess the cost versus the value of the services being provided. On occasion you will find that the pure cost of outsourcing is more expensive than the anticipated costs of not outsourcing. To properly conduct the cost and benefit analysis, you should consider the tangible costs and intangible benefits. The tangible costs include quantifiable items relating to the actual goods and services being received. Examples of tangible costs are: hardware and software costs; consulting fees;

#	Requirement	Weight	Company A Score	Weighted Score	Company B Score	Weighted Score	Company C Score	Weighted Score
1	Contractual and physical ownership of all hardware and software being utilized on the mainframe, telecommunications and WAN	2	4	8	10	20	10	20
2	Support center (help desk) operations	10	10	100	10	100	10	100
3	Data center operations	10	8	80	10	100	10	100
4	Telecommunications	3	10	30	10	30	10	30
5	All wide area network management	8	6	48	10	80	5	40
6	Bar coding and data collection	3	10	30	10	30	10	30
7	All hardware and software maintenance	5	10	50	10	50	4	20
8	Application development	10	10	100	10	100	10	100
9	All user training	6	10	60	5	30	3	18
10	System services personnel	10	8	80	10	100	10	100
11	Application services personnel	10	7	70	10	100	10	100
12	Application software experience	10	6	60	4	40	2	20
13	Provide business process re-engineering	7	10	70	0	0	10	70
14	Significant outsourcing experience	5	7	35	10	50	10	50
15	Large customer base	9	8	72	10	90	8	72
16	Local presence	3	0	0	10	30	7	21
17	References in the same industry as yours	5	10	50	10	50	9	45
18	Training programs for transitioned personnel	10	10	100	9	90	10	100
19	Global telecommunications network in place	4	10	40	10	40	10	40
20	Backup and recovery procedures utilization	10	8	80	9	90	5	50
	Total Score			1163		1220		1126

Figure 5.2 Sample Weighted Decision Analysis

maintenance fees; etc. Intangible benefits are those areas that you know will add value to your company but are difficult to place a dollar value on. Examples of intangible benefits are: improved company image; stability of the outsourcing firm; using the outsourcing firm as your change agent; etc.

The cost and benefit analysis should be a simple and straightforward exercise. Beware not to compare it with meaningless and/or false information. Don't make these top two mistakes that often mar the analysis:

1. Forgetting to include the time value of money. Since you are working with a multiyear agreement, this could have a definite impact on the outcome of the analysis.
2. Failure to account for the risks inherent in the outsourcing process. Where possible, the risks identified in the risk assessment should be valued and considered as appropriate.

Risk Assessment

Risk Assessment is a systematic thinking process for uncovering and dealing with potential problems that are reasonably likely to occur and damaging if they do. Risk Assessment asks two basic questions: What could go wrong? What can we do about it now? Four basic activities provide the framework for the Risk Assessment:

1. Areas of vulnerability are identified. Where could we be most deeply hurt? At what points could change affect us most heavily?
2. Specific potential problems are identified within the areas of greatest vulnerability. These are specific situations that pose such a serious threat that immediate action is required.
3. Actions are identified that will prevent occurrence of specific potential problems. These actions are directed at the likely cause of the threatening problem.
4. Contingent actions are identified that can minimize the effects of potential problems that cannot be totally prevented.

Risk Assessment should not be thought of as a negative search for trouble. Rather, it is a positive search for ways to avoid and reduce risk that is likely to come in the future. As such, Risk Assessment is one of the most rewarding activities that your Outsourcing Team will engage in. It provides individuals and organizations with their best chance to build the future in accordance with their visions and desires. Risk assessment is one of the finest tools available for bringing into focus today the best thinking of an informed management team properly concerned with the future. An example of a Risk Assessment is provided in Figure 5.3.

Confidence Assessment

The Confidence Assessment is a tool to help you assess your confidence level with one company compared to another. For the most part, this assessment is a subjective analysis that provides a means to document your concerns and "gut" feelings. It is possible for an outsourcing firm to meet all the requirements and fare well in the previous analysis, and still you may have a hunch that their capabilities might not meet your expectations. An example of this may be the caliber of the personnel representing a specific outsourcing firm whom you have met. You may feel as though the chemistry isn't right between your company and the outsourcing firm even though there are no hard facts to support the suspicion. Documenting these concerns in a formal process allows you to compare concerns across multiple outsourcing firms.

To help understand the result of a Confidence Assessment, you may want to score each concern. The score, which can be either weighted or not, would be used to compare one firm with another. A low score would indicate a higher confidence level with the specific outsourcing firm. This analysis can also be combined with the Risk Assessment analysis.

The analysis/assessment tools described above are just a few of the methods for assessing the outsourcing firm's capabilities. The outcome of these analyses can be of great value from this point forward in the outsourcing process. As another benefit of these tools, the Cost and Benefit analysis and the Risk Assessment will generate valuable information that will most likely be presented to the Board of Directors (or appropriate management group) for their approval of the overall outsourcing contract.

To aid in the proposal evaluation process, you may want to enlist the assistance of a third-party consultant. As mentioned earlier, the third-party consultant can bring valuable insight to your proposal evaluation process. Consultants that have worked with the various outsourcing firms can quickly point out the strengths that one outsourcing firm has over the other. Using a consultant will help to decrease the amount of time needed to evaluate the proposals and help to reduce your overall risks.

Category	Risk	Risk Abatement
Technical personnel	The entire IS staff will be transitioned to the outsourcing firm, and they will not be obligated to return to the company at the end of the contract.	The contract will clearly state that the outsourcing firm personnel working on the company's account will be allowed, if they desire, to transition back to the company at the time of contract termination. The contract will state specific guidelines that the outsourcing firm must follow, should there be a transition back to the company.
Contract duration and termination	The proposed 10-year term poses a risk, should business conditions or priorities change during that period.	The proposed agreement is a partnership, not a typical supplier/customer relationship. Per the contract there will always be an "out" for breach of contract or non-performance. In addition, the company will have the right to renegotiate the contract in the event of a significant change of business (e.g., ownership change, major acquisition or disposition, etc.)
Contract scope disputes	As it is not feasible to identify all tasks and duties that the IS organization currently performs, nor is it possible to fully anticipate the future projects or activities of the existing IS staff, the potential exists for disagreement regarding in-scope vs. out-of-scope work.	The company will retain the responsibility for assigning priorities to all outsourcing firm tasks. Additionally, all work will be "within scope" as long as it can be performed with the agreed upon full-time equivalent (FTE) resources. The outsourcing firm will also be responsible for meeting the IS performance service levels established by the company.
Technical skills of personnel	As IS technology changes and the company's business needs vary, the company will require a variety of technical skills. While we can confidently project the skill mix requirements for the next year or two, it is not feasible to think that we can identify the skill mix that will be needed in later years.	The contract will be structured for the outsourcing firm to commit a negotiated number of FTE technical personnel to the company. This will ensure that a constant level of competent technical support is maintained at the company throughout the life of the contract.

Figure 5.3 Risk Assessment

At this point, the Outsourcing Team is definitely at a major milestone for the overall outsourcing process. It is time to make the final decision as to whether to outsource or not. Once you have completed the proposal evaluations, your Outsourcing Team will have most likely accumulated a great deal of knowledge about your current Information Systems environment and the areas needing improvement. This newly acquired knowledge should be used to make a final recommendation to the executive staff. The recommendation should be one of four possibilities:

1. Implement a full outsourcing agreement
2. Implement a partial outsourcing agreement
3. Do not outsource but make changes as appropriate
4. Do nothing — leave the Information Systems environment as it is

Let's take a detailed look at each of the four possibilities.

Implement a Full Outsourcing Agreement

During the outsourcing process, your team has been convinced that outsourcing all of Information Systems is the right strategic move for the company. The outsourcing firms have been successful in convincing the team that outsourcing the entire Information Systems responsibilities would be a cost-effective way to meet future requirements without jeopardizing the quality of information system-related services to the organization, its customers, and suppliers.

Implement a Partial Outsourcing Agreement

The Outsourcing Team feels your company will benefit from outsourcing only a portion of the Information Systems responsibilities. Normally this decision is based on the desire to outsource the portions of Information Systems that are considered to be either an area of weakness, high risk, or too costly to maintain. The Outsourcing Team should identify which areas should be outsourced versus those that should be retained. It would also be advisable at this time to address how both the outsourcing firm and your company's Information Systems organization would coexist to form a workable solution.

Do Not Outsource But Make Changes Where Appropriate

This operation would indicate that the Outsourcing Team is confident that it would not be in the best interest of the company to outsource. However, during the outsourcing process, the team has concluded that there are areas for improvement that should be addressed. The team should be ready to highlight each area in need of improvement and its potential impact on the overall company.

Do Nothing — Leave The Information Systems Environment As It Is

While it is not impossible, this is an option that rarely occurs. By recommending the status quo, the Outsourcing Team states that it sees no room for improvement in the Information Systems environment. This would be an enviable position for any Chief Information Officer. By making this recommendation, you are saying that you are the best in the world and the entire industry is following your lead! Give this option considerable thought before recommending it to your executive staff.

Summary

Having completed the proposal evaluations and determined what your recommendation to the executive staff will be, it is time to select the winning bidder. (This assumes your recommendation is to implement a full or partial outsourcing agreement.)

By using the tools described here, as well as other methods your Outsourcing Team might have decided to use, you will select the winning bidder. This bidder should be notified, and the schedule for contract negotiations should be established. The bidder that comes in second should be told where they stand, and that you would like to leave the final decision open, based upon the completion of successful negotiations with the selected bidder. In doing this, you will leave the door open with the number-two bidder in the unlikely event you and the selected bidder are unable to reach an agreement. This will provide the Outsourcing Team an opportunity to revisit the runner-up bidder before deciding on the next course of action. This rarely happens, because building a partnership takes a willingness to work together and both giving and taking are required to make the partnership successful. However, it is always nice to know you have another option in the event it is needed.

The proposal evaluation process is key to the success of an outsourcing agreement. Take your time and enlist support from industry experts and internal personnel to do a thorough review of the proposals.

6 | Contracts

B y this point in the process you will have an excellent understanding of exactly what you expect to achieve by outsourcing. You have defined your requirements and you have selected an outsourcer that you feel will best meet those requirements. However, your work is far from over. The contract you will be developing, between the outsourcer and your company, will be an instrument that must survive for the term of the contract. Since outsourcing partnerships are multiyear contracts, the contract must be well defined. It must be written in a manner that assumes those who initially developed and approved the contract may not be the same individuals who will be working together in the future. Therefore, it is imperative that all agreements be documented. It is often said that, if everyone does their job properly, once completed and signed the contract is placed on the shelf and seldom, if ever, referred to. But as we all know, this is rarely the case. Changing business requirements over time and personnel turnover will necessitate referring to the contract to ensure that both parties are functioning within the scope of the contract.

It is for these reasons, and of course to establish legal responsibility, that a contract be established which clearly defines responsibilities and liabilities. There are three general rules of thumb when writing the outsourcing contract. First, you should control the document and be responsible for changes and updates as appropriate. It has been proven that "he who owns the document controls the process." In addition, you do not want to be tied to the outsourcer's timetables. Instead, you need to update the contract and word it so it is most beneficial for your company.

The second general rule is to use language that is easy to understand and is unambiguous. Don't forget that while you and your Outsourcing Team may be the authors of the contract, you certainly will not be the only ones who will have to read and interpret the contract over the life of the agreement. As such, you should use clear and simple language that is easy to understand and does not require a lawyer's interpretation. As you can imagine, the contract will most likely be a large document when completed. During the process of developing the contract it is easy to repeat something you have already said in another section, although it may not be worded exactly the same way. In doing this, you introduce the possibility for confusion and ambiguity that could cause problems in the future. Therefore, it is important that you describe and define each portion of the contract and ensure that the information is not repeated elsewhere in the contract.

The third general rule of thumb is to have a Statement of Work (SOW) as an addendum to the contract. This would create a structured document where the legal language is separate from the technical language. The main body of the contract would consist of topics such as liabilities, remedies, penalties, termination clauses, payment schedules, warranties, and other areas necessary for legal representation from both companies. The Statement of Work, however, is dedicated to the technical description of the actual work to be performed. It is in this section that you define the day-to-day responsibilities, performance measures, Service Level Agreements, actual hardware and software to be used, etc. In addition, this provides an easy way for various personnel to be involved in the contract development process without having to understand both the technical and legal aspects of the agreement. The individuals assisting would focus on the portion of the document that is appropriate for their field of expertise.

Adhering to the Outsourcing Model defined in Chapter 1, you should now have the information and details required to start to develop a comprehensive contract. You will find that the majority of the information presented in Chapter 4 will be required as part of the contract. Information regarding specific hardware, software, data center operations, security, etc., will all need to be specified in the body of the contract. A sample outline of an outsourcing contract is provided in Appendix D. As you can see, the contract must address all aspects covering an Information Systems organization. In effect, you will be writing the instrument that will merge two companies together to form the partnership. As a result, you must ensure that you have adequately addressed each topic of concern and provided means to resolve any potential issue or dispute that may arise in the future.

Throughout the contract there is specific contractual language that should be addressed. A portion of this information is standard and can be found in many business contracts. In addition to the standard items, there are specific items that deal with outsourcing which should be included. A partial list of these items, standard and outsourcing-specific, that should be addressed in the contract is provided for your review in Figure 6.1. Since all items are important, they are listed in random order and their sequence does not imply importance.

Figure 6.1 provides the majority of clauses that should be included in the contract. The clauses followed by an asterisk (*) are particularly important for Information Systems outsourcing contracts. Further details and the intent of each clause are discussed in the following pages. It should also be noted that examples and comments about specific contract clauses and language are intended to represent samples and/or suggestions for each contract clause noted. Actual wording of the clauses for your company should be created by your Outsourcing Team and internal legal staff or their appointee.

List of Facilities

A list of facilities should be provided which identifies all buildings, offices, factories, warehouses, etc., that will require support during the outsourcing agreement. In addition, each facility's address should be provided as well as specifics about each facility. Specific information such as square footage, number of floors, etc., should be provided where appropriate. The list of facilities should also contain (at a minimum) the following information for each facility on the list:

- A brief description of the facility
- The primary purpose and use of the facility
- Number of employees located at the facility
- Number of shifts the facility runs
- Current Information Systems software applications being utilized to support the operational and administrative environment of the facility
- Any known future expansion of the facility
- Any software or hardware enhancements, including local area network, that need to be addressed at the facility

Site Access

The contract should be very specific about the regulations, policies, and procedures regarding access to each site and/or facility. To adequately provide

- List of Facilities
- Site Access
- Notices
- Description of Services
- Confidentiality
- Service Levels
- Costs and Charges
- No Solicitation
- Auditor Access
- Governing Law
- Response Time
- Staff to Be Assigned*
- Staff Caliber
- Contract Termination*
- Equipment Leases
- Site to Be Used
- Indemnification
- Backup System Availability
- Backup Files and Programs
- Taxes
- Adjustments to Charges when Volume Changes*
- Business Termination

- Account Manager (or Project Manager)
- Processing Priority
- Third-Party Service Contracts
- Rights to Security Inspection
- Change Procedure – Programming
- Change Procedure – Processing
- Force Majeure
- Verification of Costs
- Liquidated Damages for Delay
- Data Ownership*
- Information Technology Council
- Customer Obligations*
- Reliability Parameters and Standards
- Continuity During Dispute*
- Arbitration
- Quality Standards
- Security Procedures
- Price Protection*
- Ownership of Data Center (and Other) Assets
- Disaster Recovery Procedures*
- Term of the Agreement
- Default and Termination

- Non-Compete
- Transitional Services
- Notice of Automatic Renewal
- Evidence of Insurance
- Maintenance
- Correction of Errors
- Distinguish Between Outsourcer, Customer, and Third-Party Systems*
- Hiring of Employees
- Transfer of Personnel
- Payment Schedule
- Adjustment to Charges for Overtime
- Relationship
- Media Ownership
- Miscellaneous Expenses
- Designation of Authorized Representative
- Miscellaneous Services to Be Provided
- Limitation of Liability
- A Guarantee That Your Costs and Services Are Equal or Better than Other Customers*
- Amendments

Figure 6.1   Contract Considerations (*Denotes special importance for IS outsourcing contracts.)

support, the outsourcing service provider would need to have access to the majority of sites and facilities. Where special security is required, this should be noted in the contract. For highly secured areas, you may also want to require the outsourcing service provider to designate specific individuals who will be responsible for secured areas. In the event your company provides products and/or support services to the U.S. government or other international governments, you may also want to require the outsourcing firm to provide personnel with a specific security clearance. It would also be appropriate to state in the contract that personnel requiring access to the secured sites will be required to sign a security agreement prior to your company authorizing access to the secured facility.

Notices

Throughout the contract you will be addressing various topics that will need to be formally communicated between both contracting parties. In order to ensure that these communications are received by the appropriate personnel, the contract should specifically identify to whom (by organizational title, office, and address) the notice should be addressed. This specific notification clause should be specified for both contracting parties. Specific information should be provided that spells out where notices are to be delivered for your company and the outsourcing firm. Addresses, telephone numbers, company position, and if appropriate, specific names should be included for both companies. Doing so eliminates the uncertainty of where to send a notice and to whom it should be addressed.

Description of Services

It is extremely important to be very thorough in this section of the contract. Specific descriptions of services must be provided which clearly identify the services the outsourcing firm will be performing. In order of magnitude, this section can potentially be the largest section of the contract. The description of services should include detailed explanations of the services along with the appropriate performance measures and performance goals. Many times the description of services portion of the contract contains a general definition of the type of services to be provided. For further details about the services to be provided, this section generally refers to the Statement of Work.

As mentioned, the Statement of Work is an attachment to the contract and is dedicated to describing the technical requirements of the agreement.

Examples of services descriptions are as follows:

Application Services. The term "Application Services" means all activities associated with requirements maintenance, trouble-shooting, and documentation of all software applications supported by the outsourcing firm's account team. The term includes, but is not limited to, systems services, computer systems, the local area network, the wide area network, the Internet and Intranet, data collection systems, bar coding systems, telephone switches, and all supported personal computer software. The term also includes support for business application issues such as investigation of problem causes, applying corrective action, providing Information Technology consulting as required, and business applications training.

System Services. The term "system services" means all activities associated with daily operations, user administration, new installations, maintenance, cabling, hardware, and systems software for current computer systems and their peripherals, and system software for the local area network, the wide area network, Intranet, associated peripherals, and the telephone system. The term also includes daily operation of the help desk and end-user training for office automation software.

Security

You will want to ensure that the outsourcing firm complies with the written security procedures that are in effect at your facilities as of the effective date of the contract. You may also, if applicable, want to indicate that your company will provide all necessary security personnel and related equipment for the security requirements while on your company's property.

Confidentiality

It is highly likely that the outsourcing firm will be exposed to confidential company information. As a result, it is important to address confidentiality requirements in the contract. Specific language should be developed that prevents the outsourcing firm's employees from disclosing any confidential information about your company. It also should be worded in such a way that the outsourcing firm itself would be liable for any breach of confidentiality. An example of a confidentiality agreement is as follows:

> With respect to financial, statistical, and personnel data relating to your company and the outsourcing firm's business which is confidential, is clearly so designated, and which is submitted to one company from the other in order to carry out this Agreement, the receiving company will instruct its personnel to keep such information confidential by using the same care and discretion that they use with similar data which is designated as confidential within their own company. However, your company and the outsourcing firm shall not be required to keep confidential any data which is or becomes publicly available, is already in their possession, is independently developed by your company or the outsourcing firm outside the scope of this Agreement, or is rightfully obtained from third parties.

Service Levels

Service levels are primarily used for clearly defining the level of service or service performance that is expected from the outsourcing service provider. The service levels should include specific performance measures that will be used to determine if the service provider is meeting the goals and expectations as set forth in the contract. Examples of service performance goals are:

- Percent of problem calls that were closed during the initial call to the help desk or user support center
- Length of time to perform telephone or voice mail adds, moves, and changes
- Number of problem calls closed during a specified time frame
- Percent of programs developed on time and within budget
- The amount of time, expressed as a percentage, that the Local or Wide Area Network is available for a given time frame. This is often referred to as the Availability Rate
- The amount of time, expressed as a percentage, that the mainframe is available for a given time frame
- Lines of code developed by programmer
- The results of the business process improvement efforts as compared to the expected results

- Number of user devices downtime occurrences
- Cost containment by function, and as a total, for Information Systems
- Number of job reruns
- Network and mainframe response time
- Number of reports distributed behind schedule

These service levels should be divided into areas such as applications development, network management, telecommunications, operations management, business process re-engineering, etc. For each category, the service levels and goals should be specially defined with current measures and target goals over a period of time.

Costs and Charges

As with any contract, the costs and charges should be explained and defined in detail. To best illustrate the costs and charges it is common for the contract to have, as an attachment, a detailed spreadsheet which provides a line-item by line-item cost detail by month, quarter, year, and contract total. Included in this section would be costs associated with personnel, facilities, equipment, maintenance for hardware and software, research and development, depreciation and amortization, subcontracting, voice and data telecommunications, travel-related expenses, office supplies, etc.

Since an outsourcing agreement could cover an extended period of time, i.e., several years, it is generally desirable to tie the amount of cost increase per year to the Consumer Price Index (CPI). This allows both companies to have a level of control to ensure that the cost of the contract is proportional to the Consumer Price Index year after year.

While there are other methods that can be used to establish a nonbiased method to control the level of price increases, the Consumer Price Index is one of the most common. This is typically done by establishing an agreement between the outsourcing firm and your company that states the amount the Consumer Price Index is allowed to fluctuate before having an effect on the price of the contract. The effect could be either negative, generating additional cost, or positive, generating a cost savings, for your company. For example, as long as the Consumer Price Index stays within a specified range, as defined when the contract was signed, there would be no changes. However, in the event the Consumer Price Index exceeds a specified threshold, the contract price would be adjusted by a predefined amount. The amount of increase is generally expressed as a percentage.

Other areas of consideration for the costs and charges section are performance-based bonuses for superior performance and penalties for poor performance. Bonuses for superior performance should be clearly defined. The definition of the bonus should state exactly how the performance will be measured. Time limits are also generally defined that identify the window of opportunity for the outsourcing firm to earn the performance bonus.

Since the vast majority of costs in a typical outsourcing agreement are related to your company (the company receiving the services), it is common to find that most managers do not think about the fact that the outsourcing firm could also incur nonreimbursable costs. An example of this would be performance-based penalties. Performance-based penalties are related to the outsourcing firm meeting specific performance goals such as project completion dates, systems availability rates, cost reduction goals, etc. It is highly advisable to include performance-based penalties that clearly state the cost to the outsourcing firm in the event that they do not meet the specific performance goals.

One cost-related area to pay close attention to is the cost for terminating existing leases. If you have leased hardware and/or software and you plan on transitioning the leased assets to the outsourcing firm, there will most likely be an early termination fee that you will have to pay if you decide to proceed with transitioning the asset to the outsourcing firm. For this reason, hardware and software often remain as "retained" assets until such time as it is no longer cost prohibitive to terminate the lease.

Other areas for cost would include the expense of transitioning employees back to your company at the end of the outsourcing contract, legal fees, and utilities costs.

No Solicitation

During the term of the contract you may want to limit the outsourcing service provider's ability to solicit additional business. While you do not want to harm the relationship between the outsourcing firm and your company by strictly forbidding the service provider from promoting additional business, you may want to limit the amount of solicitation that would be permitted. A way to deal with this is to have any new proposed business be presented through a common source within your company. In this manner you have one person, or office, that is responsible for evaluating business proposals by your outsourcing service provider. You may also want to prevent or control the amount of solicitation via third-party service providers through your outsourcing service provider. Care should be taken in this area to find a balance that allows your outsourcing service provider the ability to promote additional business but have the proper controls in place to prevent the outsourcing firm from overextending their capabilities and losing sight of the original goals of the outsourcing agreement.

Auditor Access

Since outsourcing agreements are normally very large and involve millions of dollars, it is highly likely that both the outsourcing firm and your company will want to have the right to have independent auditors review the financial information and project-specific financial statements. Doing so will help to ensure that both companies are operating within the guidelines of the contract and financial arrangements. Assuming both the outsourcing firm and your company are publicly held companies, this should not be a major issue. However, if one or both of the companies are privately held this can sometimes be a very sensitive issue that must be addressed. Care should be taken to ensure that both parties clearly understand the auditing requirements and auditing frequency for both your company and the outsourcing firm. There should also be a clear procedure developed that specifies what should be done when a discrepancy is found.

Governing Law

It is highly likely that the outsourcing firm's corporate offices are in a different location than yours. Therefore, it is important to agree on the state and local jurisdiction that would take precedence in the event of any legal action by either party. It is highly recommended that, since your organization would stand to have the highest risk, combined with the fact that you are the customer, the governing law be defined by your company.

Response Time

The response time for both systems and services required from the outsourcing firm is a critical area that should be monitored closely to ensure that the service provider is responding in a timely fashion. Response times should be divided into several categories. A few of the categories may be:

- System response time for:
  - Mainframe
  - Network
  - Help desk
  - Support during normal work hours and evenings, weekends, and holidays
- Problem identification and resolution
- Time required to adjust the Information Systems staff in accordance with upturn and downturn of your market or business in general

At a minimum, it is essential to clearly define the response times associated with each of the above categories. There may be other response time categories that are necessary for your specific business. If this is the case, they should be included in the contract as well. Care must be taken to define realistic response times and ensure that they are documented in the contract. It is important to determine the appropriate response times during the negotiation phase of the outsourcing process because it would be more difficult to establish or change the expected response times after the contract has been signed.

Staff to Be Assigned

Assuming you are transitioning your Information Systems employees to the outsourcing firm, it is appropriate to specifically address the staff that would be assigned to your company in the contract. Without this right, the outsourcing firm can replace and/or assign personnel to other locations as they desire. In a partnership agreement, you have to trust the outsourcing firm to do what is best for your company. Therefore, you must ensure that the outsourcing firm personnel working for your company have the skills, attitude, and experience that best suit your needs. You also want the right to approve or disapprove any assignment made by the outsourcing firm's Account Manager. In addition, this section of the contract can be structured to ensure the employees being transitioned to the outsourcing firm will be treated fairly and professionally.

Staff Caliber

While you would expect the outsourcing firm to place only the most highly qualified personnel on your account, this isn't always the case. Clearly it would be the outsourcing firm's desire and intention to place the best personnel on every account they have. However, due to strong resource demands, and in some cases high personnel turnover rates, outsourcing firms are forced to place personnel that are not as qualified as you would like. To ensure that the personnel assigned to your account have the qualifications you desire, you should be very specific in the contract about the qualifications required for outsourcing staff personnel. These qualifications can be years of experience, a college degree within a specific profession, experience in specific technology, length of time in your industry, etc.

If you elect to place this section in your contract you should have specific qualifications for each primary area of responsibility. For example, you would not have the same qualifications for a programmer analyst as you would for a database administrator, network administrator, telecommunications analyst, etc. Regardless of the number of requirements you define or the number of interviews that you conduct, there will always be the potential for a person to be assigned to your account who does not meet your expectations. As a result, you should specifically state in the contract that, upon request by authorized personnel, any employee of the outsourcing firm will be replaced with an individual more suited for the position.

A few companies have gone as far as to require that each outsourcing staff member be interviewed and approved by designated company representatives. Interviewing each individual would only be feasible for smaller outsourcing agreements. It would not be practical for outsourcing agreements that involve hundreds of outsourcing personnel.

Contract Termination

In any contract you will generally find several sections that address termination for cause. In the event either party does not perform as expected and does not meet the requirements of the contract, the other party has the right to terminate the agreement. The termination for cause is important and must be addressed to ensure that you have the right to terminate the contract in the event either party fails to deliver the services or goods as specified in the contract. Rarely do you see, nor would you expect to see, a clause specifying the right to terminate for convenience. Due to the long-term nature of outsourcing agreements, companies are reluctant to sign an agreement that locks them into a partnership for a time frame as long as 10 years.

Typical outsourcing agreements are 5 to 10 years in duration, with the most common being 10 years. As a result, many companies feel a strong reluctance to contractually obligate themselves for that length of time due to the uncertainty associated with the business environment. When you think about it, it is virtually impossible to predict what will occur in your specific business over the next 10 years. Therefore, you can see how easy it is to be reluctant to contractually obligate yourself for that length of time. With few exceptions, this should be considered one of the high risks associated with outsourcing. An effective way to address this situation and minimize your risk is to include a termination for convenience clause.

Termination for convenience is just that. It provides you with the ability to terminate the contract for no justifiable reason. It is conceivable that over the course of many years your company may decide that, while the outsourcer is meeting the conditions in the initial contract, you may have a strong desire to terminate the agreement and regain ownership of the activities that were originally outsourced. While it is difficult to address specific examples as to why this action may be taken, termination for convenience does provide a means to negate the risk for the long-term agreement.

The primary purpose for the termination for convenience clause is to assure the Board of Directors and shareholders that you have a way to terminate the contract regardless of the reason. However, if the outsourcing decision was based on the right reasons and outsourcing became part of the company's strategic focus, then it is highly unlikely this clause would ever be enacted.

When negotiating the termination for convenience clause, the outsourcing firm will most likely insist upon a penalty fee and reimbursement of actual expenses associated with terminating the contract. The penalty fee should be prorated and reduced as the contract matures. It is also reasonable to assume that the outsourcing firm will insist on limiting the right to enact the termination for convenience clause to specific years during the life of the contract. For example, in a 10-year agreement, the contract may be structured in such a way that at the beginning of years three, five, and seven, you will have the right to exercise the termination for convenience option. The contract should also be structured to ensure the decision to terminate for convenience is reviewed by the Information Technology Council for their approval.

Equipment Leases

With the financial advantage associated with leasing, it is very common today for a company to have multiple leases for both hardware and software systems. This creates an issue when you consider outsourcing. For example, if the hardware and software that is being leased is to be transferred to the outsourcing company, the lease will most likely have to be bought out. As a result, either your company or the outsourcing firm will be required to pay the cost to terminate the lease. Due to the potential of high penalties, it is sometimes better to wait until a future date to terminate the lease. In this event, the contract should clearly state when the lease will be terminated and, if appropriate, when the assets will be transferred to the outsourcing company.

If the leases are to be terminated as part of the initial outsourcing agreement, the contract should be very specific about how the leases for the hardware and software will be terminated and who is responsible for following through on the transactions.

Site To Be Used

If your Information Systems organization is consolidated, it would be appropriate to specify the site that the outsourcing personnel will use as their offices. Also included in this section would be the actual site that will house the data centers. In the event that your company's Information Systems resources are spread throughout your organization at multiple sites, you may want to designate one of the sites as the official office, or headquarters, for the outsourcing personnel.

Indemnification

As a rule, indemnification is an area that should be given close consideration while developing the contract. Since the outsourcing firm will have access to your company's data and may be responsible for processing the data, they are in a high-risk situation. We all have heard stories and may have personally been involved with systems issues that have corrupted databases and caused significant damage to a specific business. As a result, the outsourcing firm will normally want to be indemnified against the loss of data or business interruption due to systems errors. What is actually right or proper for your company can only be defined by you and your legal staff. Care should be taken to closely examine the potential for damage, loss, business interruption, and related risks.

Backup System Availability

After outsourcing the Information Systems responsibilities, it is highly likely that you will no longer have day-to-day operational control of your systems environment. As a result, you should define your expectations and requirements for systems backup and associated availability in the event of a system outage. For mission critical applications, the applications that are essential to run your business, you may want to insist that the outsourcing firm maintain a "hot site." The hot site is a fully functional backup system that is ready to go online at a moment's notice. For less critical applications it may be appropriate to require a "warm site" or a "cold site," each of which can be ready for system processing within a predefined period of time. For example, a cold site will typically require two to four days of preparation once a disaster has been declared.

The business resumption, or disaster recovery, planning is often an area that is overlooked by Information Systems organizations. This however, should be a major area of focus in your overall strategic Information Systems planning process. It only takes one disaster for you to realize the importance of having a good Disaster Recovery Plan and the devastation that can be caused by not having one. This is something you can require the outsourcing firm to do for you, or it can be contracted through a third-party service provider. The bottom line is that without a Disaster Recovery Plan, with contractual obligations associated with it, your company is exposed to significant business interruption risk with overall data damage and loss.

Backup Files And Programs

It should be a standard course of business to perform functions such as backing up your files and programs. However, as we all know you should never assume anything when it comes to writing a contract. As a result, requirements for backing up files and programs should be explained in detail. You should also require the outsourcing provider to develop a full backup procedure including the use of an offsite storage facility, with associated documentation.

The backup procedure documentation should clearly define the exact procedures that specifically identify what is to be done, when it is to be completed, and who has the responsibility for performing the procedure. The procedures should also be controlled documents and be maintained in a centralized area. The file and program backup system should include a daily backup of files with no less than weekly backup for the entire system. To highlight the importance of this procedure, it should be clearly documented that the backup procedure will be subject to internal audits without notice.

Taxes

Depending on the type of outsourcing service provided, you may be required to pay state, federal, and local tax. To assist you in determining the services that are taxable, it would be appropriate to require the outsourcing provider to provide line-item information that separates taxable versus nontaxable services on its invoice. This should be discussed in detail with the outsourcing provider during the contracting phase, being sure that the result of the discussions and decisions are documented in the contract itself. Doing so eliminates unpleasant surprises in the future.

Adjustments to Charges When Volume Changes

As you develop a pricing structure with the outsourcing firm, you will want to ensure that as the volume of work changes throughout the term of the contract you will have the means to adjust the price accordingly. In all likelihood the first two to three years of the contract will be defined, and both you and the outsourcing firm will understand exactly what is expected. However, over the life of the contract it is impossible to predict exactly what your requirements will be from a personnel and services standpoint. As a result, you and the outsourcing firm will do your best to predict what those requirements will be and price them accordingly. As the future unfolds, your assumptions may or may not be correct. Therefore, you will want to have the right to adjust your cost, usually on an annual basis, to reflect the services to be performed over the next 12 to 24 months.

Business Termination

Since the majority of outsourcing contracts span many years, it is appropriate to address the issues associated with business termination. No one enters an outsourcing agreement thinking that the business or the relationship will be terminated prematurely. However, with the length of time involved, keep in mind that key decision makers for both your company and the outsourcing firm will most probably change. As a result, it is impossible to foresee what effect the change in business, marketplace, competition, etc., will have on the viability of your company. If the 1980s and 1990s have taught us anything, it is that companies are bought and sold all the time, regardless of their size and position in the marketplace. History has taught us that no company is immune from corporate buyouts.

When considering this, combined with the fact that no one can predict the future, you must assume the worst when writing an outsourcing contract and ensure that your company has the legal right to terminate the contract in the event your company is acquired or goes out of business. As a result, you will want to have the flexibility to manage the contract up to and including termination as appropriate. As described herein, you will want to have the right to terminate the contract for cause as well as convenience.

Account Manager (or Project Manager)

In order to have a single point of contact with your company, the outsourcing firm will normally assign an Account Manager. The Account Manager will be responsible for the day-to-day operations as well as the long-term relationship between your company and the outsourcing firm. As a result, the Account Manager will be a key individual you will rely on heavily to ensure the success of the outsourcing process. Given the critical nature of this position, it is advisable that you include an option in the contract allowing you to approve who will be the Account Manager assigned to your company. It would also be advisable to include language that allowed you to request the Account Manager be replaced in the event the individual does not meet your expectations. You will also want to be very specific about the qualifications required for the position. A few recommended qualifications would be:

- Specific industry experience related to your business
- At least 10 years of experience with the current outsourcing firm
- Served as an Account Manager on another account that the outsourcing firm allows you to contact if desired

The outsourcing firm knows that it is in its best interest to assign the best possible person to the account. But regardless of how qualified an individual is, the fact is there are times when he/she is just not right for your company.

It is also advisable to require the outsourcing firm to identify the Account Manager prior to signing the contract. This allows you to interview the Account Manager and understand his/her background prior to making the commitment with the contract. Once you've identified the individual you feel comfortable with, you may want to include the individual, by name, in the contract. Going a step further, it is also advisable to include this individual in the contract negotiations so that he/she will understand the circumstances that led to each specific agreement in the contract. This will actually save time and reduce the level of potential conflicts in the future.

Processing Priority

In some cases outsourcing agreements include moving the customer's computer room assets to a shared data center controlled by the outsourcing firm. Doing so will mean that the personnel responsible for your data processing needs will be scheduling your actual data processing along with several other companies' processing schedules. In this event, you will want to ensure that your processing needs have the proper priority as compared to the other customers that the outsourcing firm is managing. To address this issue it is advisable to include in the contract the priority you expect the outsourcing firm to use. Examples would be a timetable developed for critical operations management processes and business applications such as material requirements planning, cost roll-ups, daily, weekly, and monthly processing.

Third-Party Service Contracts

While the need for third-party consulting services should be significantly reduced after outsourcing, it is still highly likely that you will need additional services along with those already being provided by the outsourcing firm. There are three ways to accomplish this:

1. Requiring the outsourcing firm to establish the third-party services contract
2. Identifying and entering into an agreement for third-party services yourself
3. A combination of both

Your outsourcing agreement should clearly state that any third-party contracting must be approved by the Contract Administrator or the person responsible for interfacing with the outsourcing Account Manager. In the event the outsourcing firm selects the third-party service provider, you may also consider requiring the outsourcing firm to "pass down" specific contract clauses to the third-party service providers for which the outsourcing firm has a legal commitment. Doing so can ensure that specific contract clauses, i.e., confidentiality agreements, security rights, etc., will be passed along to any third-party service providers that the outsourcing firm elects to use.

Another point to consider is whether or not you want the outsourcing firm to be responsible for the actions of a third-party service provider. If so, this needs to be clearly stated in the outsourcing agreement.

In the event that you may want your company to select a third party to assist in your systems operations, it would be appropriate to allow the outsourcing firm to approve your selection. You should have the right to use any third-party service provider you want. However, the outsourcing firm, as your new partner, may object to your specific decision. As a result the outsourcing firm should have the right to disagree with your decision in writing and ask the Contract Administrator to resolve the associated issues. Regardless of the outsourcing firm's reason for the objection, the Contract Administrator should have the final decision in the matter. If the outsourcing firm Account Manager feels strongly about the objection, he/she may elect to elevate the issue to the Information Technology Council for consideration and final resolution.

Rights To Security Inspection

Since the outsourcing firm will most likely become the keeper of the data, it is advisable to evaluate or inspect the security of the outsourcing firm on a regular basis. While I am sure you would never outsource your data systems to someone with whom you do not feel comfortable, it is still a good idea to verify the level of security.

When addressing security, you should think about it in two different areas. First is the physical security, for example, access to the data center and actual hardware. Second is "virtual security." This is security in terms of systems access, database and application-specific security, etc. I would advise you to include in the contract the right to inspect the physical and virtual security at any time. I would also advise you to follow through with the inspection at least twice a year. Areas to consider for inspection would be:

- Network access
- Mainframe access

- Facility access
- Computer room access
- Database administration procedures
- System administration procedures
- Telecommunications access
- Personnel authorized to access systems

Change Procedure — Programming

If your agreement includes outsourcing application programming services, you will most likely not have day-to-day operational control of the programming staff. As a result, it is advisable to include in the contract a change procedure for the outsourcing firm to follow when making changes to existing software. The contract should clearly state that the initial programming change procedure, as documented in the contract, can be updated at any time upon the concurrence of the outsourcing firm's Account Manager and your company Contract Administrator. The initial change procedure should include the entire process from notification of a need for a change through, and including, implementing the change with associated training and documentation updates.

The majority of outsourcing firms have excellent change procedures and would be happy to implement their own change procedures at your company. However, it is advisable to review those procedures in detail to ensure that you agree with them, and so state that in the contract. If you don't agree, you should work with the outsourcing firm's Account Manager to establish the change procedures that would be acceptable for both the outsourcing firm and your company. Upon reaching this agreement, the procedure should be documented in the contract.

Change Procedure — Processing

As with programming changes, you can be assured that during the term of the contract there will be various and numerous processing changes required. An example of this would be the month-end close process. If you decide to change the sequence and/or timing of processing for the month-end close, this will have to be coordinated with the outsourcing firm. In most cases, your processing will be done in a shared environment. As a result, the outsourcing firm must coordinate any changes in processing with multiple customers.

The bottom line is you are not concerned with the outsourcing firm's other customers, but only desire to have your processing environment managed to best fit your business needs. Therefore, you should have a detailed processing change procedure documented in the contract that clearly illustrates the process for implementing processing changes. The processing changes should include all steps within a normal process change with signature approvals required at the appropriate points. Again, you'll want to clearly state that the processing change procedure can be changed with the approval of both the outsourcing firm's Account Manager and your Contract Administrator.

Force Majeure

Both you and the outsourcing firm will most likely want to include statements in the contract protecting yourselves against issues and liabilities associated with force majeure events. Both parties will want to include language that relieves them of responsibility in unexpected and uncontrollable events such as storms, floods, tornadoes, etc. It is expected and understood that the outsourcing firm cannot be held responsible for disasters as a result of natural acts. However, it does not relieve them of the responsibility for ensuring a timely and well-orchestrated recovery from the event. This section of the contract should clearly state that in the case of a force majeure event, the outsourcing firm is expected to declare a disaster and respond as identified in the contract.

Verification of Costs

During the term of the contract, there may be times when you question the outsourcing firm's invoice or would like to verify the cost being reported. This is especially the case in a Cost Plus, or anything less than a firm fixed-price contract. You'll want to ensure that the contract provides the right for your company to verify the costs being reported by the outsourcing firm at any time upon your request.

Liquidated Damages for Delay

With today's companies becoming more and more dependent upon computer systems to run their business, it is very common to find companies that absolutely depend on having systems available during critical times of the day. An example would be in a retail business where customer orders are taken over the telephone. The success of this environment depends on the computerized order entry system and the telecommunications system being functional and available during normal operating hours. As a result, the contract should clearly state that in the event of delays for reasons other than force majeure, there will be a potential for penalties that the outsourcing firm must pay. The contract should be very specific about what would qualify as an action resulting in the outsourcing firm needing to pay a penalty fee. The contract should also specifically identify how the penalty fee would be calculated and in what length of time after the event it would have to be paid.

Data Ownership

The information stored in your company's data files is considered to be the "keys to the kingdom." Without these data it would be extremely difficult, if not impossible, to run the business. For this reason, the fact that your company will retain total ownership of your data should be clearly established in the contract. Regardless of where the information resides, whether it be at an outsourcing firm's processing center or data center(s) located on your own property, you must retain legal ownership of the data.

As you are entering your new partnership with the outsourcing firm, no one expects or anticipates the worst case scenario in which: the partnership does not work; disputes erupt; and legal actions are taken against each other. But the fact is, this does happen on occasion. In the unlikely event that this would occur, you do not want to give the outsourcing firm the ability to hold your data "hostage" pending settlement of any dispute between your two companies. Therefore, a properly structured contract will specifically state that you will retain ownership of the data, even though the outsourcing firm is responsible for processing the data.

Information Technology Council

The Information Technology Council's primary objective should be to ensure the overall partnership between your company and the outsourcing firm is a success. The Information Technology Council is used as a committee that:

1. Provides overall guidance for the Information Technology direction of your company
2. Ensures the positive relationship between your company and the outsourcing firm
3. Serves as a review board for any disputes that may arise

The contract should clearly state that the Information Technology Council consist of key executives from each company. Due to the potential for personnel changes over the term of the contract, it is best to identify the representatives of the Information Technology Council by position rather than actual names.

Customer Obligations

Throughout the document, the contract is structured toward specifying what the outsourcing firm will do for you. Since this is truly a partnership being developed, it is appropriate to dedicate a section in the contract that specifically addresses what your company's obligations are during the term of the contract. In a partnership, the outsourcing firm cannot be successful without your company's assistance. During the outsourcing process, the outsourcing firm has gathered information about your company and has decided that the partnership would be a good business venture. Otherwise, they would not be negotiating the contract. They are taking a risk and are assuming that your company will continue to be successful in delivering the services and items which were agreed to during the course of the negotiating process. Therefore, the contract identifies the responsibilities that your company will be accountable for over the course of the contract. Examples of this would be: appointing a member of senior management to be the focal point for the outsourcing Account Manager; providing office space and supplies; prioritizing utilization of resources; ensuring the outsourcing firm is aware of your strategic direction; etc.

Reliability Parameters and Standards

In the event you require specific hardware reliability parameters and standards, they should be specified in the contract. These standards and parameters can be related to mainframe processing, network processing, engineering workstations, test equipment, etc. While it is not common-place, some companies will assign reliability performance requirements to selected software applications as well. In this event, the software reliability requirements should also be stated in the contract.

Both hardware and software reliability parameters should be specific by component type or module, software module, location, etc. It is also helpful to include these parameters including a clear description of what constitutes a failed parameter.

Continuity During Dispute

The contract should specify the procedures for identification and resolution of any disputes from either party during the term of the agreement. Regardless of how good the partnership is, it is reasonable to assume that during the life of the contract there will be disputes that will need to be resolved. Since the outsourcing firm is controlling a key element of your business, Information Systems, you must ensure the proper contract language is established so your business is being adequately run during the dispute process. This area is closely tied to the issues described in the "Data Ownership" section above, but should be expanded to include personnel and data processing, along with data ownership. Having this risk covered in the contract will ease the dispute resolution process and ensure your company is not at risk during the process.

Arbitration

Since the typical scope of an outsourcing agreement is very large and extends over a multiple-year period, it is appropriate to assume that at some point in time during the term of the contract, a need for arbitration will exist. There is no question that the issue should be resolved at the lowest possible level in the organization, but in reality this is not always possible. The problem resolution hierarchy should be the outsourcing firm's Account Manager and your company's Contract Administrator, followed by the Information Technology Council, followed by arbitration. The contract should clearly state the terms for arbitration and that once an issue goes to an official arbitrator both companies will abide by the arbitrator's decision. The contract should also state that the arbitrator will be a third-party, impartial individual or panel.

An example of an arbitration procedure section is:

> Any dispute, controversy or claim arising out of or related to this outsourcing contract, or the creation, validity, interpretation, breach or termination of this contract, and the parties are unable to resolve through informal discussions or negotiations through other alternative dispute techniques, will be submitted to binding arbitration using the following procedure:

1. The arbitration will be held in the place selected by the party initiating the arbitration proceeding, before a panel of three arbitrators. Either party may provide a statement of the dispute, controversy, or claim, and the facts relating or giving rise thereto, in reasonable detail, and the name of the arbitrator selected by it.
2. Within 30 days after such demand, the other party will name its arbitrator, and the two arbitrators named by the parties will, within 60 days after such demand, select the third arbitrator.
3. The arbitration will be governed by the Commercial Arbitration Rules of the American Arbitration Association, except as expressly provided in this Section. However, the arbitration will be administered by any organization mutually agreed upon by the parties. If the parties are unable to agree upon the organization to administer the arbitration, it will be administered by the American Arbitration Association. The arbitrators may not amend or disregard any provision of this Agreement.
4. The arbitrators will allow such discovery as is appropriate to the purposes of arbitration in accomplishing fair, speedy, and cost-effective resolution of disputes. The arbitrators will reference the rules of evidence of the Federal Rules of Civil Procedure then in effect in setting the scope and direction of such discovery. The arbitrators will not be required to make findings of fact or render opinions of law.
5. The decision of and award rendered by the arbitrators will be final and binding on the parties. Judgment on the award may be entered in and enforced by any court of competent jurisdiction.

The above is just a sample of how the arbitration section of your contract may read. The actual language should be developed by your Outsourcing Team and your company's legal representatives.

Quality Standards

With quality standards such as ISO9000, QS9000, MS9000, M1003, etc., being required in today's marketplace, it is advisable to also require your service provider to be, at a minimum, Information Systems-ISO9000 certified. You may also want to implement your own quality certification program where, on a predefined time basis, you would requalify the outsourcing service provider to ensure they are meeting your standards. You may even want to drive the quality standards down to an individual design and program quality level. Each phase of the design effort and each program must meet predefined quality measures established by your company. These standards and quality requirements are best enforced if they are included in your contract. It is also advisable to develop quality measures where you track the outsourcing firm's quality performance on a regular basis.

Requiring the outsourcing firm to track the Cost of Quality (COQ) is another means to measure the performance of the services being received. The actual cost elements that would be included in the Cost of Quality calculation should be consistent with what your company uses in other Cost of Quality measures.

Security Procedures

Since the outsourcing firm will have the potential to have total control of your company's electronic information, it is essential that you understand and agree to their security procedures. This focus should not only be on the physical security, such as building and data center facility access, but also security from an electronic standpoint, such as virtual security which was discussed earlier. In this age when electronic commerce is expanding greatly, security procedures must be in place to ensure that only authorized personnel have access to your information. Where feasible, you will want to have security to the lowest level possible in your system processing and system access areas. As a result, it is advisable to ensure that the contract clearly states that your company has the right to inspect security procedures and where appropriate request the security be strengthened.

Price Protection

The long-term nature of an outsourcing agreement involves multiple years of service. When negotiating the price for the contract, the outsourcing firm will most likely request that you agree to pay for any inflation over the term of the contract. This is not an unreasonable request but one that should be addressed by linking the inflation rate to an appropriate national standard such as the Consumer Price Index (CPI), as discussed previously. Further, you should consider having the outsourcing firm absorb the increase of inflation for the first few percentage points (e.g., up to a 5% change over any 12-month period, and share equally in the increased expense of the amount exceeding 5%). In this case, the contract would be structured so that if the Consumer Price Index exceeds 5% change in any 12-month time frame you will agree to pay one half of the cost exceeding 5%. In doing so, you share the burden of cost containment with the outsourcing firm and agree to share in the risk of out-of-control inflation. This method is particularly helpful for a fixed-price contract and will also assist you in determining fair increases for a Time and Materials or Cost Plus contract.

Ownership of Data Center (and Other) Assets

If the actual data center is included in the outsourcing agreement and the outsourcing firm moves the data center to its own facility, there is no question that it owns and controls that data center. However, if the outsourcing firm will retain your data center either in the existing location or move it to another location in your company, then the question of ownership becomes an issue that should be addressed in the contract. Many companies retain the actual ownership of the data center, assuming the data center is on their property, and rents or leases the facility to the outsourcing firm. Other companies choose to retain ownership and provide use of the facility at no charge to the outsourcing firm, while yet others insist that the outsourcing firm move the data to the outsourcing firm's location. The contract should clearly state who has physical ownership of the data center and all the equipment (and software) located in it.

In addition to the data center assets there are other assets such as:

1. Personal computers
2. Network equipment
3. Software
4. Printers
5. Data collection devices
6. Terminals
7. Test equipment
8. Tooling

These items should also be clearly designated as being owned by the outsourcing firm or retained by your company. This is a tedious task to go through but important to the overall success of the agreement.

In the same light, you should also clearly define how the acquisition of new equipment will be addressed. For example, the outsourcing firm can purchase the equipment for a fee, you can purchase the equipment through funds from your own company and allow the outsourcing personnel to use it, the equipment can be leased from either party, etc. All of this should be thought through, decided upon, and documented in the contract.

Disaster Recovery Procedures

With the threat of disaster, natural or otherwise, that exists for all companies, it is amazing the number of companies that do not have a viable Disaster Recovery Plan. For those companies that do have a Disaster Recovery Plan, you should ensure the outsourcing firm will either assume the responsibilities of maintaining the plan or at the very least be assured by them that they will follow your plan in the event of a disaster. If you do not have a current Disaster Recovery Plan, the contract should specifically address how this will be resolved in the near future. Perhaps you would prefer developing your own Disaster Recovery Plan or ask the outsourcing firm to develop the plan for you. Either way, the plan must be developed. The outsourcing firm should also agree on the disaster recovery procedures and contractually agree to ensure that they are followed. This should be structured so that failure to do so would constitute a breach of contract which, in turn, would provide your company a right to terminate the contract for cause.

Term of the Agreement

The term of the contract should be clearly stated and discussed in detail. In addition to the term of the agreement itself, this section should also include a detailed discussion about options for renewal at various points throughout the contract life. It is strongly advisable to include renewal options at various points during the contract term. This allows you to assess the true business value of the outsourcing agreement, during different times of the contract term.

An example of this section would be as follows:

> The term of this Agreement (the "Term") will begin on January 1, 1998 (the "Effective Date") and will continue until the fifth anniversary of the Effective Date, subject to earlier termination in accordance with the Termination Section of the contract. The Term shall automatically be

extended for successive one-year periods (the "Successive Terms") there-after, unless at least six months prior to the end of the original Term or a Successive Term, either party notifies the other that the Agreement will not be so extended. The date on which the Term expires due to passage of time is referred to in this Agreement as the "Expiration Date." This Agreement may be terminated prior to the Expiration Date in accordance with the Termination Section.

Default and Termination

Given the overall size of the outsourcing agreement, it is appropriate to provide detailed specifications that define what constitutes contractual default and the various types of termination clauses that may or may not be associated with contract defaults. Defaults and terminations are discussed further throughout this text.

Noncompete

Since the outsourcing firm will have access to your company's proprietary data, it is appropriate to include a noncompete clause in the contract. The noncompete clause should be specific and list the names of companies considered to be your competitors and request the outsourcing firm not do business with these firms. This can simply be a list of company names as an attachment to the contract. Depending on your specific industry and environment, you may want to also include noncompete clauses for personnel working on your account. This would limit your exposure and ensure that personnel working with company proprietary information would not be in a position to work with one of your competitors.

Transitional Services

Depending on the scope of the outsourcing agreement, the transition of your processing services to the outsourcing firm could be a very significant event. The transition will most likely involve relocating the data center, while making personnel changes in your Information Systems organization. Moving the data center must be a carefully planned event. Done properly, this process would include full contingency planning steps in the event a problem was encountered during the physical move of the data center. In order to reduce risk, the move is often contracted out to a third-party service provider that specializes in this type of activity.

As discussed herein, transitioning the personnel to the outsourcing firm can be a very traumatic and emotional event. As a result, it would be wise to schedule the transition of personnel first. This allows the Information Systems personnel time to get acquainted with their new company and work environment. Only after this milestone is achieved would I recommend moving the data center. The risk is too high if you try to move the data center and transition the Information Systems personnel at the same time.

During this transitional phase the outsourcing firm must ensure that your company's data are protected and there is no interruption of your business. As a result, it is appropriate to include in the contract language that will clearly define the scope of the transition and specific milestones associated with the transition. If third-party services, such as hardware relocation assistance services, will be used for the transition, care should be taken to ensure that the outsourcing firm has the liability for the success of the transition. This liability should apply regardless of whether it is the services being provided from their company or third-party service providers.

Notice of Automatic Renewal

Many outsourcing contracts are written with an automatic renewal option. This provides the ability for the contract to be automatically renewed by a specific date unless notice by either party is given by that date. This is particularly common with contracts that are shorter in duration. Automatic renewals are an easy way to extend the contracts but can also be a detriment if not properly managed. Assuming the relationship between the outsourcing firm and your company is good, having an automatic renewal allows you to extend the contract for a given period of time with little or no effort. However, if the relationship between you and the outsourcing firm is less than desired, then the automatic renewal, if forgotten about, can cause legal problems. It is often said that if an outsourcing partnership is working well, the contract is rarely referred to. As a result, over time, it is easy to forget about specific clauses in the contract, such as automatic renewal. There certainly isn't anything wrong with having automatic renewals in the contract; it is just something that both parties need to be aware of, and should not be forgotten about over time.

Evidence of Insurance

To be certain that both parties have adequate business insurance, it is appropriate to contractually require both companies to produce evidence of insurance upon request. Your company, at a minimum, will most likely be required to have evidence of insurance for personal injury while outsourcing personnel are on your property. The outsourcing firm, however, will most likely be required to have much more extensive insurance coverage. Since they will have the primary responsibility for processing your company's information, you should require them to have insurance for areas such as business interruption, disasters, and personal injury. Another point to consider is the amount of insurance that you require your outsourcing provider to carry. It is common to mandate that for the term of the agreement, the outsourcing provider will guarantee insurance coverage up to a specified dollar amount. The actual amount should be stated in the contract.

Maintenance

Since the outsourcing firm will be assuming all or a portion of your hardware and software responsibilities, you should ensure that the methods, policies, and procedures for maintaining the equipment and software are clearly specified in the contract. Hardware and software maintenance is typically provided in a year-by-year contract agreement and normally paid on a monthly basis. A good rule of thumb is whoever has the responsibility for supporting an application or area should also have the responsibility for the maintenance of the associated software or hardware. Therefore, depending on the scope of the contract, it is conceivable that the maintenance requirements will be shared by both your company and the outsourcing firm. Regardless of who has the responsibility for maintenance, it is essential that the responsibility be clearly defined in the contract. Doing so will eliminate many issues in the future.

For maintenance for which the outsourcing firm is responsible, you may want to require the outsourcing firm to ensure that maintenance contracts with third-party providers are renewed annually. This would be the standard way of maintaining third-party contracts unless otherwise approved and documented by your company's Contract Administrator.

Correction of Errors

To help each company keep track of error correction, it would be appropriate to document the error correction policy and procedure in the contract. This provides a guideline for both companies to use when an error is found and requires action. Guidelines and procedures should be established, not only for system-related errors that are discovered after the contract signing, but for contractual errors as well. It should be clearly documented that the contract change procedure is to amend the existing outsourcing agreement.

Distinguish Between Outsourcer, Customer, and Third-Party Systems

Prior to outsourcing, the types of software used are limited to two types, the in-house software (or custom developed) and purchased software (from an outside supplier). Once you have started the journey of outsourcing, you will now be introduced to a third type of software, the outsourcing firm software. The contract should be very specific in terms of your company's rights, as well as those of the outsourcing firm, with regard to each of the three types of software.

You must also review each current contract with your existing third-party suppliers (including hardware suppliers) to ensure you have the proper authority and permission for the outsourcing personnel to use the software or hardware that you may currently be leasing. In the event your company does not have the authority to grant the outsourcing firm permission to use the software, you must resolve the issue prior to signing the outsourcing agreement. Otherwise you run the risk of having an outsourcing agreement in place only to find that your Information Systems staff is not authorized to use the software.

Hiring of Employees

Since both the outsourcing personnel and personnel from your own company will be working together on a daily basis, it is common to find a situation where a manager would like to hire an employee who is currently working for the other company. In order to ensure a good partnership, it is highly recommended that this practice be forbidden or highly discouraged for both your company and the outsourcing firm. Many companies will include language in the contract that prevents one company from hiring employees from the other. At times the contracts will further state that, upon termination from one company or the other, a specific employee cannot work for the other company within a specific period of time, i.e., one year.

Transfer of Personnel

While it is normally the intent of the outsourcing firm to assign personnel to your account on a permanent basis, there are always those cases where, either by their choice or your choice, personnel are transferred to and from your account. This is a normal practice and done properly should cause no interference with day-to-day operations. However, it is advisable to provide contract language that states that upon your request, and if the outsourcing firm's Account Manager agrees, an individual (or individuals) would be transferred from your account. On the other hand, if the outsourcing firm desires to transfer an individual, you should insist on having approval authority before the transfer takes place.

Over an extended multiyear outsourcing agreement, it is difficult to manage the delicate blend of having the right personnel assigned to your account at the right time. Nonetheless, everyone wants to be fair to an individual and, where possible and feasible, permit the individual to transfer if desired. However, to maintain a stable environment, you cannot have a revolving door when it comes to personnel assigned to your account. Nor should you allow a revolving door for your personnel that are working with the outsourcing firm. To prevent this from happening in either company, it is best to state clearly in the contract exactly what the policy is for personnel transfers. Included in this statement is a definition of any associated limitations and procedures that must be followed.

Payment Schedule

To ensure there are no disputes, a payment schedule should be developed that specifies on a monthly basis the exact amount that will be paid each month to the outsourcing firm for the term of the contract. Included in this schedule would be any bonuses with the caveat that the outsourcing firm meet the objectives as defined in the contract. The payment schedule should also clearly define any potential event that would alter the payment schedule. An example of this would be increase or decrease of the CPI on which the outsourcing firm's rates are based.

Adjustment to Charges for Overtime

We all know that it is impossible to predict the exact amount of work (labor hours and specific skills) required to develop new systems as well as maintain existing systems for an extended period of time. As a result, many companies provide some flexibility when it comes to labor rates, even in a fixed-price contract situation, for the cost of labor. One area that you may consider for flexible rates is the area of overtime. In the event the outsourcing firm does pay their employees overtime, it may be appropriate to provide contractual language that limits the amount of overtime that you will be willing to reimburse. Another way to address this issue is that you will only reimburse for overtime that has been preapproved by the Contract Administrator. While there are other ways to address the overtime costs, it is up to you and your organization to define the controls and limits that best fit your specific environment.

Relationship

The relationship section of the contract should clearly define the relationship between your company and the outsourcing firm. An example of this section is:

> When the outsourcing firm provides services to your company, it is acting only as an independent contractor and under no circumstances will the outsourcing firm be deemed to be in any relationship with your company carrying with it fiduciary or trust responsibilities, whether through partnership, joint venture, or otherwise. Neither party undertakes by this Agreement or otherwise to perform any obligation of the other, whether regulatory or contractual, or to assume any responsibility for the other's business or operations. Each party has the sole right and obligation to supervise, manage, contract, direct, procure, perform or cause to be performed, all work to be performed by it hereunder unless otherwise provided herein.

In addition to the above, it would also be appropriate to define all known relationships between third-party companies, the outsourcing firm, and your company.

Media Ownership

Depending on many factors, such as privately or publicly held companies, size of the company, the role that Information Technology plays in the strategic positioning with your competition, etc., you will most likely want to control the information being released to the media, such as newspapers, professional publications, etc. As a result, it is very common for companies to want to control the content and timing of information that is released to the general public. This does not mean that the outsourcing firm shouldn't be allowed to release information, but does imply that the information and timing of its release must be approved by your company prior to release to the media. Since outsourcing can potentially impact large numbers of personnel, timing of the release of information to the media is critical. Premature release of information to the media can cause many problems that are difficult, and sometimes impossible, to overcome. Therefore, it is essential that both parties agree on who is responsible for the release of information and the procedure by which the information will be released.

Miscellaneous Expenses

Throughout the term of the contract there will be miscellaneous expenses required by the outsourcing firm. Expenses such as office supplies, postage, books, subscriptions, etc., are examples of miscellaneous expenses that the outsourcing firm may encounter. Without question, the best way to address miscellaneous expenses such as these is to require the outsourcing firm to absorb the cost of miscellaneous expenses within their standard rates. However, if deemed appropriate, you may want to have the outsourcing firm bill these expenses on an as-incurred basis. As mentioned, if the outsourcing firm is being reimbursed for miscellaneous expenses, it is advisable to require the outsourcing firm to provide line-item detail in both their initial proposal and subsequent monthly invoices.

Designation of Authorized Representative

Regardless of the size of the outsourcing agreement, it is essential that you have representatives that are designated as the primary points of contact for both companies. These individuals are authorized to make decisions on behalf of both companies and have a clear understanding of the guidelines by which they must operate. It is also important that a procedure be developed for each company to use in the event you need to change the authorized representatives. Typically the authorized representatives are, at a minimum, the Account Manager for the outsourcing firm and the Contract Administrator or the Chief Information Officer for your company. Regardless of who you select as your authorized representatives, you must ensure that they are involved in the outsourcing partnership and have a clear understanding of the day-to-day issues. It also should be well documented and posted as to who the authorized representatives are for both companies.

Miscellaneous Services to Be Provided

During the outsourcing process, you should be very thorough in defining the specific roles and tasks to be performed by the outsourcing service provider. Regardless of how thorough you are, there will always be miscellaneous services that will need to be performed on an as-needed basis throughout the term of the contract. To avoid contract scope issues in the future, it is wise to acknowledge the fact that there will be miscellaneous tasks required for the outsourcing firm to perform at the direction of the Contract Administrator. This is generally not an issue as long as the miscellaneous tasks do not require additional resources, and hence, do not increase the outsourcing firm's costs of operations. Regardless, the contract should provide a means for your Contract Administrator to authorize miscellaneous services.

Companies will often place a dollar limit on the miscellaneous services section. The dollar limit should be based on single event, annual total, and contract term total. Miscellaneous services costs that exceed the approved limits would typically require a contract amendment.

Limitation of Liability

It is standard practice for each company to limit the amount of risk and liability associated with the contract. Generally, the outsourcing firm will want to limit their liability to the amount for which they are being paid by your company. In a typical outsourcing agreement, the outsourcing firm will acquire a large amount of responsibility whose overall value far exceeds the amount that they will be invoicing your company. This, coupled with the fact that the outsourcing firm will be controlling the large majority of your company's data, places the outsourcing firm in a position that could potentially do a great deal more damage than the value of the contract itself. For example, if for whatever reason, the data center was not accessible by your customers, your suppliers, or internally to your own organization for several days, how much damage would that accumulate? The exposure is very real and should be addressed accordingly in the contract. This does not mean the outsourcing firms are high-risk companies to work with. Assuming you select a top-rated outsourcing firm, the risk is very low. But this does not mean that there is no risk involved. As a result, it is best to provide the understanding, up front, with the outsourcing firm and ensure that the liability agreements are documented in the contract.

A Guarantee That Your Costs and Services Are Equal to or Better than Other Customers'

Since all outsourcing agreements are unique, it is extremely difficult, if not impossible, to compare the price for the services being received from the outsourcing firm. To ensure you are receiving the best possible price, and to avoid risk of overpayment for services received, you should put the burden of proof on the outsourcing firm. Hence, the outsourcing firm should contractually agree to make the commitment that the price being charged to your company is the same as for any of their customers receiving similar services. The outsourcing firm should also be required to allow an auditing agent of your choice verify, at any time during the term of the contract, that this is the case.

Amendments

Since the term of the contract is normally several years, it is feasible that there will be amendments required to the contract. As a result, a procedure should be developed that clearly documents the process of changing the contract.

Summary

The sections above represent thoughts and suggestions on how to deal with specific outsourcing issues when developing the contract. The intent of this information is not to provide official legal advice, but to provoke thought and raise issues that may otherwise be forgotten. Although many of the sections do not provide great detail, that does not mean that one is less important than the other. The actual level of importance and the amount of detail provided for each section is clearly a function of the specific agreement between your company and the outsourcing firm. At a minimum, each area addressed in the sections listed in Figure 6.1 should be covered in the contract.

To assist in the contracting process, I highly recommend engaging outside legal counsel. With the amount of money and risk involved in an outsourcing agreement, it would make sense to have legal experts assist you. A well-written contract is a key factor in ultimately deciding whether or not the partnership is a success. There are a few legal firms today that specialize in outsourcing contracting. The attorneys in these firms deal with outsourcing issues every day, while in all likelihood this is the first time that you and your company have addressed this type of contracting. Therefore, it would be in your best interest to retain the assistance of an expert to, at the very least, review your contract prior to any finalizing of the agreement with the outsourcing firm.

Another area in which the outsourcing legal counsel could assist you is in the negotiation of the contract. Since they are experienced in this type of negotiation, they will be able to assist you in identifying which negotiation strategies will work best for your specific requirements and business environment. They will also be able to save you time when it comes to reaching an agreement with the outsourcing firm, because they will know what is and is not acceptable to the outsourcing firm.

The contract is the most important document associated with outsourcing. Without a well-written and well-structured contract you will most likely not have a successful partnership. It should be everyone's hope and goal that once the contract is signed, it becomes a document that is rarely reviewed to resolve an issue. If you truly have a good relationship with your outsourcing partner, issues will be resolved, the daily operations will run smoothly, and your companies will grow and profit together without having to rely on specific contract language to guide you through the process.

Due to the long-term nature of outsourcing agreements, it is likely that personnel will change in both companies during the life of the contract. As a result, the contract will be the only true means that both parties have to determine the intent of the partnership and the guidelines and boundaries that they must work within. When writing the contract, great care should be taken to ensure a well-thought-out and organized agreement that gives both parties room to operate freely without having to constantly refer to the contract in order to achieve a highly successful business partnership.

7 Negotiations

Negotiating an outsourcing contract should be a structured and thoroughly planned process. While the typical "do's and don'ts" of negotiating certainly would apply, you are going to need an experienced and highly skilled Negotiating Team to effectively negotiate on your company's behalf. This is primarily due to the fact that you begin the process with a large disadvantage. In all likelihood, the outsourcing firm is already aware of your actual cost history and future cost projections. As a result, you will find this aspect of the outsourcing process becomes particularly frustrating.

By this point in the process you have "bared your soul," when it comes to your Information Systems current financial status, to the outsourcing firm. This was necessary to fully assess the viability of outsourcing and to convince your company's executive management that it is in their best interest to outsource. By now you have also found that the outsourcing firm is like any other company when it comes to disclosing financial information. They will not disclose their anticipated profit margins nor their pricing strategy to you. As a result, they literally know everything about your Information Systems organization, your company, and the Outsourcing Team members. On the other hand, you know very little, if anything, about their financial profit and loss for your specific account. What it all really boils down to is *price versus value*.

The first thing to remember is that this partnership has to be a value-added partnership for both companies. You cannot expect the outsourcing firm to lose money on the contract nor can the outsourcing firm expect you to pay more than your current spending level without adding value. The best you could hope for is that the outsourcing company makes money, your company spends less than you are currently realizing, and that your overall

- Define the right Negotiating Team

- Know the company you are dealing with

- Define your expectations

- Define your limitations and weaknesses

- Develop a cost model

- Develop the negotiating strategy

- Know your bottom line

Figure 7.1   Negotiating Model

level of Information Systems service improves. If this is not the case, then something has gone wrong somewhere in the outsourcing process.

An effective approach to negotiating can be accomplished by establishing the negotiating process in the proper sequence of events. Illustrated in Figure 7.1 is a Negotiating Model that has been used successfully in outsourcing contract negotiations. By following the proven steps in the Negotiating Model, it can be used as a tool to help achieve the best possible agreement for your company.

Let's take a close look at each of the steps in the Negotiating Model and see how each can be used to achieve the desired results.

Defining the Right Negotiating Team

Typically the Negotiating Team is made up of selected members from the Outsourcing Team. The Negotiating Team should have no more than four members and should include your Chief Information Officer and a representative from your legal staff. Team members should also be extremely familiar with the intent of the outsourcing process and have a thorough understanding of your business. Additionally, all Negotiating Team members must have extensive experience in negotiating contracts. This is not the type of contract that you would want a novice negotiator involved with. You are, in effect, turning the company's information over to your new business partner and you want to ensure that your most highly qualified personnel are chartered to negotiate the best arrangement possible.

It is also common to see outside legal counsel (specializing in outsourcing) as a member of your Negotiating Team. Care should be taken when you have outside legal counsel. You should get them involved early in the outsourcing process to ensure they are fully aware of what the issues are and have a detailed understanding of your company. By the time you reach the negotiation phase of the outsourcing process, your outside legal counsel should have already drafted a recommended approach for positioning your company at the negotiating table. They most likely have been across the negotiation table from the same outsourcing firm you are negotiating with. They will know what to expect and how far they can push the associated issues with the outsourcing firm.

A disadvantage to having outside legal assistance in the negotiating room is the outsourcing firm may be unwilling to give up something knowing that they may be meeting with the same legal counsel in the future while working on another outsourcing deal. The outsourcing firm will be concerned about setting a precedent and may think twice before buying into a specific resolution. If you are using outside legal counsel and you think this may be a concern, you may want to keep the outside legal counsel out of the negotiating meetings and in the background for consultation and advice.

The Negotiating Team should also have an individual appointed as the person who will have the final say in any topic to be discussed. This is something that you normally would not want to advertise to the outsourcing firm. The team should function as a team, everyone participating equally and fairly. The designated person of authority can make the decision during private discussions without the outsourcing firm representatives being present, thus not revealing who the real decision maker is.

Know the Company You Are Dealing With

To successfully negotiate a contract, you must know the people sitting across the table from you. You should have a good appreciation of their strengths and constraints. To the best of your ability, determine how much they are willing to change without jeopardizing the success of the partnership. During earlier steps of the outsourcing process, you should have conducted several reference checks on the outsourcing firm that you are about to negotiate with. Conducting the references checks is an excellent opportunity to learn as much about the outsourcing firm as possible. While performing the reference checks, it would not be appropriate for the companies you were talking with to disclose their specific contractual agreements with the outsourcing firm. However, you can still gain a good appreciation for specific positions that the outsourcing firm may have on issues related to your company.

By the time you are at the negotiating table you will have spent several months talking with the outsourcing firm's representatives and should have developed a professional relationship in which you feel comfortable. As a result, you should now have a good grasp of what is important to the individuals and the areas in which they are most likely to be flexible.

Define Your Expectations

As with any other business venture, it is imperative that you establish proper and realistic expectations prior to going to the negotiating table. As a result of your research and analysis you should have a fairly good understanding of what to expect at the negotiating table. In addition, your site visits and discussions with existing customers of the outsourcer are excellent means for assessing what to expect during negotiations. Just keep in mind that this is a partnership. You cannot negotiate this contract like you would with a computer hardware supplier or Information Systems service provider. This is primarily due to the fact that the outsourcing firm is assuming a level of risk that these other suppliers are not. It all comes down to a value-added partnership.

Your expectations should be established with this thought always present. The outsourcing deal may cost more or less than you are currently spending in the Information Technology area. Regardless of the costs, there should also be value-added to your company as a result of entering into the outsourcing agreement. Failure to establish the proper expectations will lead to a very frustrating, and possibly a failed, negotiating process. This can be avoided by taking a realistic view and remembering that this is a partnership where both companies must benefit.

Define Your Limitations and Weaknesses

Having a clear understanding of where your limitations and weaknesses are provides insight for you in terms of where you are most vulnerable. By contrast, knowing the limitations and weaknesses of your business partner, the outsourcing firm, provides opportunity for you during the negotiating process. You can be assured that the outsourcing firm has already developed an approach in negotiating with you and your team. You can also be assured that the outsourcing firm has identified the areas where they feel your company is most vulnerable. Not having the same type of information on your side of the table will open doors of opportunity for the outsourcing firm, thus potentially causing a less than desirable result. Identifying your areas of limitations and weaknesses in advance gives you a chance to have a strategy for addressing each area when it comes up. While it may not happen, you should assume that the outsourcing firm will take advantage of your weaknesses to gain an advantage in the negotiating process. Knowing your opponent's limitations and weaknesses gives you ample time to prepare ways to take advantage of the negotiating process.

Develop a Cost Model

In order to determine if outsourcing could be a cost savings venture, you should have already forecasted what you anticipate your Information Systems costs to be over the next 10 years (assuming you are working toward a 10-year outsourcing agreement). Developing the forecasted costs should have been your third step in the Outsourcing Model as described in Chapter 1. By this point in the outsourcing process, you are in a position to better understand the tangible and intangible costs and benefits of outsourcing as they apply to your company.

The Cost Model, developed earlier in the outsourcing process, should be updated prior to starting the negotiation process to reflect your expectations of what your costs would be with and without outsourcing. This model should be very detailed and consist of line items by year. An example of a typical Cost Model is provided in Figure 7.2. Having the Cost Model available and thoroughly understood by the Negotiating Team provides you with the ability to simulate the "what if's" during the negotiation process.

As you can see, the Cost Model is structured to show what the anticipated costs would be of Information Systems with and without outsourcing. The Cost Model is further divided into five primary categories. These are:

1. Nonretained (or transferred) expenses
2. Retained expenses
3. Risk reduction

Projected Cost Without Outsourcing

	Year 1	Year 2	Year 3	Year 4	Year 5	Year 6	Year 7	Year 8	Year 9	Year 10	Total 10 Years
Non-Retained Expense											
Salary/Labor	1,996,288	2,076,140	2,159,185	2,245,553	2,335,375	2,428,790	2,525,941	2,626,979	2,732,058	2,841,340	23,967,649
Benefits	343,604	357,348	371,642	386,508	401,968	418,047	434,769	452,159	470,246	489,056	4,125,347
Supplies	347,082	360,965	375,404	390,420	406,037	422,278	439,169	456,736	475,006	494,006	4,167,103
Maintenance	381,972	397,251	413,141	429,667	446,853	464,727	483,316	502,649	522,755	543,665	4,585,996
Consulting	332,000	345,280	359,091	373,455	388,393	403,929	420,086	436,889	454,365	472,540	3,986,028
Utilities	149,720	155,709	161,937	168,415	175,151	182,157	189,444	197,021	204,902	213,098	1,797,554
Travel	106,860	111,134	115,580	120,203	125,011	130,012	135,212	140,620	146,245	152,095	1,282,972
Education	80,800	84,032	87,393	90,889	94,525	98,306	102,238	106,327	110,580	115,004	970,094
Sub-Total	3,738,326	3,887,859	4,043,373	4,205,110	4,373,313	4,548,246	4,730,175	4,919,380	5,116,157	5,320,804	44,882,743
Retained Expense											
Rent	1,603,508	1,603,508	1,603,508	1,603,508	912,000	0	0	0	0	0	7,326,032
Taxes	60,444	62,862	65,376	67,991	70,711	73,539	76,481	79,540	82,722	86,031	725,697
Depreciation	1,027,308	1,464,908	1,864,908	1,865,090	1,864,908	820,000	400,000	0	0	0	9,307,122
Amortization	952,056	952,056	952,056	952,056	952,056	952,056	0	0	0	0	5,712,336
Sub-Total	3,643,316	4,083,334	4,485,848	4,488,645	3,799,675	1,845,595	476,481	79,540	82,722	86,031	23,071,187
Costs Without Outsourcing	7,381,642	7,971,193	8,529,221	8,693,755	8,172,988	6,393,841	5,206,656	4,998,920	5,198,879	5,406,835	67,953,930

Figure 7.2 Outsourcing Cost Model

Projected Cost With Outsourcing

	Year 1	Year 2	Year 3	Year 4	Year 5	Year 6	Year 7	Year 8	Year 9	Year 10	Total 10 Years
Costs Without Outsourcing	7,381,642	7,971,193	8,529,221	8,693,755	8,172,988	6,393,841	5,206,656	4,998,920	5,198,879	5,406,835	67,953,930
Risk Reduction											
Estimated Risk Factor	100%	97%	93%	90%	88%	80%	75%	70%	65%	60%	
Risk Value	0	(239,136)	(597,045)	(869,376)	(980,759)	(1,278,768)	(1,301,664)	(1,499,676)	(1,819,608)	(2,162,734)	(10,748,765)
Total Anticipated Cost	7,381,642	8,210,329	9,126,266	9,563,131	9,153,747	7,672,609	6,508,320	6,498,596	7,018,487	7,569,569	78,702,695
Outsourcing Costs											
Outsourcing Firm Price	3,289,727	3,421,316	3,558,169	3,700,495	3,848,515	4,002,456	4,162,554	4,329,056	4,502,218	4,682,307	39,496,813
Retains	3,643,316	4,083,334	4,485,848	4,488,645	3,799,675	1,845,595	476,481	79,540	82,722	86,031	23,071,187
Total	6,933,043	7,504,650	8,044,017	8,189,140	7,648,190	5,848,051	4,639,035	4,408,596	4,584,940	4,768,338	62,568,000
Savings Due To Outsourcing											
Total Savings	448,599	705,679	1,082,249	1,373,991	1,505,557	1,824,558	1,869,285	2,090,000	2,433,547	2,801,231	16,134,695
Cumulative Savings	448,599	1,154,278	2,236,527	3,610,518	5,116,074	6,940,633	8,809,918	10,899,918	13,333,464	16,134,695	32,269,390

Figure 7.2 Outsourcing Cost Model (continued)

4. Outsourcing costs
5. Savings due to outsourcing

Let's take a detailed look at each category and its value in the overall process.

Nonretained (or Transferred) Expenses

The nonretained expenses are your company's current and projected costs that would be transferred to the outsourcing firm. All costs associated with the personnel, equipment, software, consulting services, and systems maintenance would be included in this section. The costs in this category are costs that your company will no longer be responsible for after the transition to the outsourcing firm.

Retained Expenses

Retained expenses are the costs that you are currently paying (or anticipate paying in the future) that will remain your responsibility after you outsource. Retained expenses may be costs that you cannot legally pass to the outsourcing firm (i.e., taxes) or costs that you elect to retain for various other reasons (i.e., depreciation on equipment that was not transitioned to the outsourcing firm). The sum of the retained and nonretained costs would be the total Information Systems costs.

Risk Reduction

Since the length of the typical outsourcing agreement is several years, it is advisable to place a value on the risk that you may encounter. This is done by using a risk factor, a value stated as a percent. The higher the risk, the lower the risk factor. For example, you and the outsourcing firm should be confident of what the costs will be for the first year of the contract. As a result, the risk factor would be 100%. This is reduced as you apply the air of uncertainty to the future. The risk value is obtained by multiplying the inverse of the risk factor by your total costs without outsourcing, thus creating the anticipated costs.

When calculating the costs that would be compared to the cost of outsourcing, you should use the anticipated costs as a basis for your analysis.

Outsourcing Costs

The outsourcing costs category depicts the sum of the outsourcing firm's proposed price and the retained expenses. The totals in this category would represent your company's total Information Systems cost for the next 10 years.

Savings Due to Outsourcing

This category simply compares the sum of the quoted (per year) price from the outsourcing firm, plus the retained expenses, with the total anticipated costs as discussed above. The result would be a savings or loss, depending on your company's specific circumstances.

When defining the Cost Model you should explain the retained expense separately from the expense being transferred to the outsourcing firm. In all outsourcing agreements there is a portion of your company expense that is retained by your company. Examples of potential retained expense are:

- Taxes
- Amortization
- Personnel salaries and benefits (for those personnel not being transitioned)
- Depreciation for any equipment that is retained by your company
- Lease expenses

Since the retained expenses are unaffected by the outsourcing agreement, this cost should be considered as part of your total Information Systems costs when comparing your costs today versus the anticipated costs with the outsourcer. Throughout the negotiation process you will inevitably move costs from the retained and transferred areas several times as you construct the final negotiated contract scope and price. By having a detailed Cost Model, where all expenses (retained and transferred) are itemized at the line-item level, you will have a Cost Model to simulate the "what if's" during the negotiation process. Having the Cost Model in a personal computer spreadsheet provides a powerful tool that can be used throughout the negotiating process. The spreadsheet allows your Outsourcing Team and, if appropriate, the outsourcing firm representatives to see the results of making changes in the scope and pricing of the potential agreement. This method has the potential of saving you many days of work during the negotiating process.

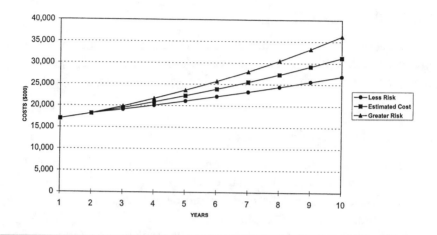

Figure 7.3   Estimated Cost Risk

To say the least, it is extremely difficult to estimate what your Information Systems costs will be over the next 5 to 10 years. You will be developing the Cost Model based on the history of Information Systems expenses and your assessment of your future Information Systems costs. It should be understood that there is a high level of risk that your estimates will not be accurate after you get past years three or four. Regardless of how well your Information Systems organization estimates their costs, what do you think the accuracy would be of developing a 10-year cost estimate? Is it feasible to think that the estimate could be off by 1%, 5%, 10%, 25%, or higher? Absolutely, there will be variables that will affect the Information Systems costs that are not known today. It should also be assumed that when you miss an estimate, it is compounded exponentially as you go forward in time. This is because many of your cost categories are based on an inflation factor of the prior year's base values. Figure 7.3 illustrates the effect this will have as time progresses. Figure 7.3 assumes an annual Information Systems cost of $17 million, with a 7% inflation factor, and a ±2% error rate (compounded annually) starting in the third year. As you can see, an annual error as small as 2% will have a profound effect over a 10-year time frame. The point of all this is, be sure you understand the value of having a good Cost Model. Take the time to get the model as accurate as possible. Always add a probability of error, or risk factor, line to the Cost Model to allow for the unknown expenses that you can be assured will happen. This factor can be found in Figure 7.2.

Develop the Negotiating Strategy

Two common traits found in successful Negotiating Teams are always having a strategy in terms of how the team will approach the negotiating process and navigating their way through the issues that are sure to be discussed before going to the negotiating table. The best way to develop a strategy is to determine what you "must have" out of the agreement and what are the desirables ("nice to haves"). This can be done by utilizing the same decision analysis tools discussed in Chapter 5, "Proposal Evaluations." Once you've decided what you must have from the negotiation process, your negotiation strategy should be developed around the "must haves."

The sequence of topics discussed is also an important part of your negotiation strategy. Typically, cost-related issues are postponed until the end of the process. This is primarily because it is difficult to assess a fair actual price until both parties are clear on the final requirements. Another common practice in negotiation strategies is role-playing. Role-playing is quite effective in that each member of the Negotiating Team understands what his/her purpose and specific role is. Examples of the roles would be:

- The typical "good guy, bad guy" scenario, where one member of the team is viewed as the one who is very demanding and inflexible. The other representative is the one who's more agreeable and, when necessary, is able to find the common ground to resolve issues. The good guy, bad guy scenario is most effective when the good guy is able to reach a point where the other side of the table has to agree, or the bad guy will have to finish negotiating a specific agreement.
- Another method of role-playing is a financial versus technical representative. This is effective because it allows each member to "play dumb" about the technical or financial aspect of the negotiations. Once this is established, the opponent usually will make comments and suggestions about the other team members. This allows team members to compare notes and help to identify where the other weaknesses are in the outsourcing firm's negotiating strategy.
- A third method of role-playing is the stubborn and closeminded person. This person would be unable to see the benefit of doing anything differently than the way he/she feels would be best. His method is normally effective only when there is a specific area that the Outsourcing Team does not want to negotiate. This person would be the one to dig his/her heels in and not give in to negotiating pressures from the outsourcing firm.

There are many roles that your team members can take to assist in achieving the results you desire during the negotiating process. The areas defined above are just three examples of the types of roles that various members of the Outsourcing Team can assume. Take the time to assess what will work best for your Negotiating Team and, if necessary, practice the roles on each other before meeting with the outsourcing firm.

Know Your Bottom Line

As defined in the negotiating strategy, you should already know what you must have when the negotiating process is completed. When it comes to the final result of the negotiating process, you should keep an open mind. Even though you have established what your bottom line is in terms of benefits and cost savings, the outsourcing firm might have offered other benefits you might not originally have thought of. In this case, you may want to substitute one benefit for another with the intent of achieving your overall goals and objectives established early in the outsourcing process. The bottom line denotes the absolute minimum of benefits, including costs, that you are willing to settle on with the outsourcing firm. It is almost assured that the bottom line you started with in your negotiating strategy will be different when the negotiations are done. It will be a give-and-take process as you form the best agreement possible.

One key ingredient in a successful negotiating process is flexibility. Assuming you have followed the steps above and developed a good negotiation strategy, there is no reason the negotiation process should be anything less than pleasant. It is often said when referring to negotiating, "Let the games begin." Of course this refers to the gamesmanship that one typically finds when negotiating. Questions such as:

- In what order should you discuss issues?
- When is it appropriate to seriously negotiate the costs?
- How high should we set our demands and what is the least we will settle for?
- What is your trump card going to be, and when is the best time to play it?
- What is our opponent's weak area and how can it best be exploited?

These and many others are examples of the questions and issues the Negotiating Team struggles with during the process.

Another important ingredient for success in negotiating is to control the environment and overall process. By developing a sound strategy and selecting the right Negotiating Team to implement the strategy, it is fairly easy to control the negotiating process. In order to control the process, your Negotiating Team must ensure that emotions do not enter into the overall process. The only time you or your team members should exhibit frustration is as a part of the strategy and role-playing you planned from the beginning. Many times it is appropriate to appoint one or two of the team members to be the more vocal individuals. As such, they would be the team members assigned to play the role of stubborn and closeminded individuals. Generally speaking, this is a common practice and one that is recommended.

An effective means of negotiating is to insist that your Negotiating Team meet frequently without the outsourcing firm's representatives. This will allow you to coordinate the process and ensure that your team is focused on the same objectives. It also sends a signal to the outsourcing firm representatives that you communicate as a team and have a logical approach to the negotiating process.

After all the business issues have been resolved and you are down to the final hours of price negotiations, it is time to reveal the person who has the final authority to close the deal with the outsourcing firm. At that time there should be one person from each company who has the authority to negotiate the final price and benefits. As the negotiations come to an end, these two individuals will usually talk among themselves to agree on the final price. This technique is successfully used by many companies but may not be necessary or appropriate for your specific situation. It is up to the Negotiating Team to determine what will work best for your company and then apply the appropriate negotiating methods and techniques to ensure a fair and beneficial contract for your company.

In summary it is essential that you have a clear and logical approach to negotiating. Your negotiations team should have a clear understanding of what their roles are and what is expected from them as individuals as well as a team. If you control the process and do not allow emotions to set the tenor of the negotiations, you will find that outsourcing contract negotiations can be rewarding and enjoyable for all parties.

8 Personnel Considerations

When existing Information Systems personnel are included in an outsourcing agreement, such as is found in the full outsourcing approach, it can be a very significant and traumatic event for both the Information Systems personnel and your company's management. In a typical full outsourcing agreement, the majority of the Information Systems personnel are transitioned to the outsourcing firm. A small percentage of the current Information Systems staff would normally be retained by your company to assist with the management and company interface with the outsourcing firm. The remaining personnel would be transitioned, laid off, or reassigned due to their position being eliminated or consolidated with similar positions. To say the least, the personnel issues become a significant challenge to your company's management team.

With few exceptions, the personnel transitioning to the outsourcing firm will have career opportunities over the long term that your company couldn't begin to provide. Outsourcing firms are in the business of Information Technology and selling technical consulting-related services. As a result, they are in a position to cultivate an Information Technology professional in the direction that is in the common good of both the employee and the outsourcing firm. For Information Systems employees who work for a non-Information Technology company (e.g., a manufacturing firm) their career is limited to the needs and growth of that specific company. With the outsourcing firm, the Information Systems employee would have an abundance of opportunities throughout his/her career and only be limited by his/her own abilities.

Since outsourcing firms are in the Information Technology services business, they must ensure their personnel are properly trained and have the opportunities to excel in their career as well as providing challenging positions. As a result, the outsourcing firm will spend a great deal more on training Information Systems personnel compared to a manufacturing company. This provides an excellent opportunity for Information Systems personnel to achieve the training and career goals which they collectively establish with their management. It also presents the outsourcing firm with the challenge of retaining the personnel they have spent a great deal of time and effort in helping to develop their careers. The outsourcing firms address this challenge by growing their business in different technologies and providing the opportunities for their personnel to achieve their career goals.

One has to speculate that if this is such a wonderful opportunity for the Information Systems personnel, why is it such a traumatic event when it is announced that your company will be outsourcing its Information Systems responsibilities? There is a multitude of answers:

- Company loyalty
- The element of surprise
- The fact that they are being told and not given a choice
- The fear of change (the biggest reason of all)

These are just a few of the reasons for this phenomenon. As an Information Technology professional myself, I find it ironic that Information Technology professionals are agents of change, but when change affects them they react as anyone else does and generally resist change. Their entire careers are based on promoting and implementing change across companies around the world. Senior Information Systems executives are well aware of the difficulty of managing change. If not done properly, regardless of what it is that's being changed, you could fail for no other reason than the lack of acceptance from those who are affected by the change.

We have built our careers on working with companies to define areas where change is required and developing methods to institute the change. With outsourcing, it is our turn to change. When managing Information Systems change, all the same rules apply and we should be aware of the do's and don'ts as they relate to effective change management. First and foremost is to have a structured plan and objective for instituting the change. If you cannot convince your peers and subordinates within your Information Systems organization that this is the right thing to do, then you don't stand a chance of convincing the rest of the company that this is a new partnership that will add value to your company's bottom line.

Surprise

Anger

Reconciliation

Acceptance

Figure 8.1   The SARA Model

Convincing corporate executives that outsourcing is the best approach for the future of Information Systems in your company can be done by demonstrating that outsourcing would result in favorable benefits and financial improvements. Assuming the benefits and financial considerations are favorable, the Board of Directors (or appropriate management) will most probably approve the outsourcing partnership. A key factor in the success of the partnership will be based on the acceptance and perceived benefits for the general work force throughout your company. Therefore, it is essential that you do an excellent job in promoting the partnership and the value that it brings to the company. This is discussed further in Chapter 11, "Partnership Management."

Regardless of how and when the Information Systems personnel are informed of the pending outsourcing partnership, you should expect a rather turbulent ride through a storm of emotions. The important thing is, have the facts ready once you inform the personnel, and keep in mind that while this may be a true benefit and a tremendous boost for the careers of Information Systems personnel, it will not be viewed that way in the beginning. You can expect each individual to go through various emotional stages. The textbook model that best describes this is the SARA model. The SARA model, illustrated in Figure 8.1, depicts four major stages that your Information Systems personnel team will go through after they are told about the outsourcing agreement.

Once the information is released, the first and natural reaction is surprise. Everybody in the Information Systems profession is aware that outsourcing is becoming more prevalent throughout the business world. But as with most things, they don't expect it to happen to them. Therefore, you receive the surprised reaction. The initial reaction of the Information Systems staff often surprises the Chief Information Officer as well. Up to this point, the Chief Information Officer has been heavily involved in the outsourcing process and obviously recognizes the associated benefits that outsourcing brings to his/her company and the Information Systems staff. As a result, the Chief Information Officer is confident that outsourcing will be an excellent opportunity for the Information Systems professionals. With this in mind, the Chief Information Officer often underestimates the impact that the initial news will have on the Information Systems staff. Often the individuals who would benefit most are the ones that have the strongest reaction. When this occurs, the Chief Information Officer is generally caught off guard. My advice is to expect the worst from each employee and be prepared for questions and reactions that are sure to follow.

The next reaction is anger, certainly the most difficult to deal with. Anger doesn't always lend itself to clear and logical thinking. It is usually a reaction caused by the lack of information and the fear of the unknown. For the Chief Information Officer, this stage of the process is a most difficult one. You still have a business to run, but you have a group of very unhappy individuals whom you have to rely on to see that the job gets done. Exercise good judgment, understanding, and perseverance while getting the facts to the personnel as quickly as possible. This will help you successfully ride out this stage of the process. Fortunately, the anger phase does not last long.

Don't make the mistake of thinking your staff is above this reaction. They are like anyone else, and it is perfectly normal to be upset about a decision that has been made for you that has the potential to profoundly affect your career. At this point in time, they have no idea of how they will be affected or whether the pending change will be positive or negative. Only time will tell. To make matters worse, the decision to outsource was most probably made without any input from the staff. As such, they view this as a major career-altering decision that they had no say in.

The reconciliation stage is the process of weighing the pros and cons on an individual basis. It is now that the Information Systems employees will start to realize that this business venture may be professionally rewarding and personally beneficial. This is also the time the Information Systems personnel will start to realize that this event is going to happen regardless of their objections. The majority of personnel develop a wait and see attitude. This is an excellent way for the Information Systems personnel to deal with the inevitable change. This is also a sure sign that they are starting to accept the pending change. It is during this phase that the Information Systems personnel start focusing on the positive aspects of outsourcing Information Systems rather than the negative.

The last and certainly the most pleasant stage of the SARA model is acceptance. As the Information Systems personnel receive the correct information, and enough time has passed for them to clearly think about the pros and cons of outsourcing, they start to accept the inevitable. At this point the Chief Information Officer has successfully guided his/her organization through the turmoil of the initial shock of outsourcing. Once everyone accepts the outsourcing decision, you can function as a team and everyone can be part of the outsourcing process. Instead of resisting change, the Information Systems employees will now be willing participants in finalizing the steps leading up to and including the completion of the transition to the outsourcing firm.

Early in the outsourcing process you should decide on how and when you will inform the Information Systems personnel of the potential fact that the Information Systems responsibilities will be outsourced. There are two schools of thought as to when it is appropriate to tell the Information Systems personnel. First is to inform them early in the outsourcing process. Second is to wait until the negotiations are completed and the contract is signed. Then inform the personnel within a few days before the actual transition is to take place. Let's further examine the advantages and disadvantages of each of these scenarios.

Informing Information Systems personnel early in the process is the exception, not the rule. Most companies decide to wait until there is a signed agreement between you and the outsourcing firm before notifying the affected personnel. However, there is a strong argument for informing the personnel early in the process and allowing them to be a part of the outsourcing journey rather than victims of it. The major disadvantage to this strategy is that it can take as long as 12 to 24 months to finalize a typical outsourcing agreement. During this extended time frame there will be instances where the outsourcing firm and your company have a very positive outlook and other times when the outlook may not be so bright. This creates an emotional roller coaster environment for the affected personnel, thus creating a very unstable environment with the potential of having a significant impact on the morale of the overall Information Systems organization. As a result, the quality of work and productivity is jeopardized. It will take good, strong leadership during this period to overcome these obstacles and to motivate your personnel to perform to the best of their abilities, even though the future of their professional careers is unclear.

Another disadvantage of informing personnel early is the increased risk of having key employees resign before the transition. A natural reaction during the first two stages of the SARA model is to find another job. Generally speaking, you can expect that approximately 10% of your Information Systems organization will resign. This generally happens from the time you first announce the intent to outsource until after the first couple of months following the initial transition. You certainly cannot prevent anyone from leaving your company prior to the transition, but you want to make sure, to the best of your abilities, that they are leaving for the right reasons. Resigning as a reaction to the outsourcing announcement is definitely the wrong reason. Every employee should give the partnership an opportunity to work, and then make the decision as to whether or not their career is headed in the direction they desire. Any time an outsourcing agreement is reached, you stand the risk of personnel resigning, but to be fair to themselves and the companies involved, their decision to leave should be made after the transition to the outsourcing firm is final.

The turmoil that is created from knowing that all Information Systems personnel could be transitioned to the outsourcing firm is a real disadvantage. It is rare in any outsourcing agreement that 100% of the Information Systems employees are transitioned. You will generally want to retain some employees to assist in managing the outsourcing activity and a multitude of other tasks. A rule of thumb on how to calculate the number of personnel who normally would be retained is: one Information Systems person for every $30 million of the total value of the agreement. Of course, this may vary depending on your specific requirements. This equation should only be used as a guideline to determine how the number of personnel you are retaining compares to other companies. Personnel not transitioning are put in a very awkward position. Until all personnel throughout your company have a good understanding of the reasons they are not being transitioned, they will be viewed differently from those who are being transitioned. The mere nature of this causes problems with morale and often jeopardizes long-term professional friendships.

While there are many disadvantages to informing the personnel early in the process, there are also advantages. First, you run the risk of someone finding out about the pending outsourcing agreement before you are ready to make the announcement. Once this occurs, the rumor mill takes over, and it is extremely difficult for your associates to distinguish between facts and rumors. This of course can cause a lot of damage to morale and senior staff credibility with the Information Systems professionals. In the event this occurs, you still have all the concerns and issues associated with outsourcing to deal with, but you also have the issue of not being trusted by your subordinates.

The biggest advantage of informing the personnel early is that the affected personnel will eventually become part of the process and, where appropriate, assist in structuring the outsourcing agreement. Therefore, the Information Systems personnel are much more likely to buy in on the whole concept of outsourcing and view the topic as a benefit to both your company and their own personal and professional interest. By the time the contract is signed and the actual transition occurs, it is highly likely that the employees will have already gone through the first three stages of the SARA model. At this point, the majority of Information Systems personnel should be in the final stage, acceptance, thereby making the transition go much more smoothly and significantly increasing the ease with which the outsourcing firm can blend into your operating environment.

Waiting until the outsourcing contract is signed to inform the affected personnel is the option that the majority of companies would choose. This is also the option I personally recommend. Since outsourcing usually is a large undertaking involving a great deal of work, money, and risk, anything can happen during the entire outsourcing process. This is especially true during the contract negotiations phase of the overall outsourcing process. Since this process can be very lengthy and can go through various on-again, off-again stages, why put the prospective transitioned Information Systems employees through the turmoil of uncertainty until you have a signed contract and all the transition details are defined. Otherwise, you will not be able to answer the majority of the questions that are sure to be asked.

By electing to inform the personnel the day before the transition, you will not escape any of the emotional reactions that you will receive from your Information Systems personnel nor will the SARA model be cut short. It is basic human instinct to feel the same surprise, anger, reconciliation, and acceptance regardless of when the information is received. The Chief Information Officer will now have the advantage of having the outsourcing firm's Account Manager to assist in dealing with these issues. Your moral and professional responsibilities are still as great as they were, but now you will have some assistance in dealing with the issues that will arise. Another advantage of waiting to inform the personnel is that they do not feel that their careers and lives are put on hold. For example, they have no reason to debate on whether they should:

- Take vacation
- Still go to the training classes or conferences that were already scheduled
- Hold off on buying new eye glasses because their health plan will be changing
- Go ahead and put their child in the private school or wait until after the transition
- Hire a replacement for the third-shift operator who just retired

Recommending this option does not mean there aren't significant advantages to counter the disadvantages. The biggest disadvantage of waiting to inform the personnel is that it creates a much more difficult time in ensuring a successful transition. One would expect that, as a result of transitioning the Information Systems services to an outsourcing firm, the rest of the company assumes they will see a marked improvement in services almost immediately. Those of us in the business realize that this is a bad assumption. To improve services requires a great deal of time and effort to ensure that the resources are focused on the proper areas to net the anticipated results.

By waiting to tell the Information Systems personnel you not only have the rest of the company looking for this immediate improvement, but you also will have a group of core Information Systems personnel going through the beginning stages of the SARA model. The combination of the two presents a management challenge to ensure that the transition is accomplished without incident and that business operations are not interrupted.

The risk of the information "leaking" prior to the outsourcing announcement is always a possibility. As discussed above, this can be potentially damaging because of the lack of factual information being disseminated. The longer you wait to inform the affected personnel, the higher the risk of the information leaking prior to the actual announcement.

Regardless of the decision as to when the Information Systems personnel are informed about the pending outsourcing agreement, you must treat it as a delicate situation, and do not think that the event is just another announcement. Whether it is right or wrong, the majority of the personnel will not take the announcement lightly. In fact, there is a high probability that this will be the most traumatic announcement they have experienced in their professional careers. It is natural to think that this type of thing always happens to the other person. As a result, when the announcement is made you must assume that it will be a surprise to everyone. To minimize the impact of the announcement, there are several things that you and your company can do to ease the tensions that are guaranteed to be created. You and the Outsourcing Team already know the benefits that outsourcing brings to your company and to the transitioned personnel. It is important to maintain a positive attitude and project an image of excitement for the event that is about to take place. Doing so you will automatically send a positive message to the Information Systems personnel as well as all company employees.

The primary cause of the fear of change is the lack of knowledge. By having frequent meetings, both group meetings and individual one-on-one meetings, you can keep the Information Systems organization informed as to the exact status of the transition. This also provides the Information Systems employees an opportunity to ask questions and voice concerns. At this time, you have the opportunity to replace rumor with facts. All questions must be answered immediately. In the case where the answer is unknown, you should note the question and inform the individual asking the question that you will respond as soon as possible.

I would also recommend having the Human Resource (HR) representatives attend the meetings to provide better response for personnel related questions. You should view your Human Resources representative as an ally and someone who can potentially defuse an emotional situation. Having Human Resources representatives involved in the outsourcing process before the announcement to the affected personnel gives the Human Resources representatives the opportunity to compare your company's existing benefits with the outsourcing firm's benefits. You will find that this information will become vital to the success of a smooth transition if it is known prior to the outsourcing announcement to the Information Systems personnel.

While it is appropriate to focus on dealing with the reactions of the Information Systems employees, you cannot forget about the reaction that your non-Information Systems personnel will have. This is an area that is commonly overlooked. For the most part, assuming the announcement is properly delivered, the remaining company employees will view the outsourcing agreement as a positive business opportunity for your company. However, there will be a few employees who will not react positively to the news. These individuals may have friends in the Information Systems department and view the pending event as something that may adversely affect their friend.

There will be those non-Information Systems employees who will view the event as a threat to their own job security. After all, if your company is outsourcing Information Systems, who is next? Everyone knows that in order to stay competitive, reduce cost, and improve quality that many companies are outsourcing all types of business. From Human Resource services to manufacturing capability, all areas can be potential areas for outsourcing. Therefore, it is normal to get positive and negative reactions from all areas in your company.

The Outsourcing Team and executive management staff should be prepared to address all employees in the company once the announcement is made. I always like to assume the worst and hope for the best. In doing so you will be prepared to handle any situation that may arise. If handled properly, there is no reason why your announcement should be viewed as a negative event for the company. There is no question that you will upset some employees, but this should not be the majority of personnel.

To minimize the impact of the outsourcing announcement, allow the outsourcing firm representatives to speak with the Information Systems personnel, both with and without the Chief Information Officer (or other representatives from your company) present. This is especially helpful when the announcement is made early in the outsourcing process. There are many questions that arise and concerns that employees have that the personnel from the outsourcing firm can address. The outsourcing firm representatives are also ambassadors for their company. They will have the knowledge and information that will help to provide a clear understanding of their company's history and current status in the market place. Assuming the outsourcing firm Account Manager has been identified, he/she should also be a part of these meetings. The Account Manager will become the person in charge after the transition is made. Once this is known by the Information Systems personnel to be transitioned, they understand that this is the individual who has to deliver the promises made by the outsourcing firm's marketing and sales representatives. The Account Manager will also be viewed as the authority figure and will be able to eliminate many of the concerns the Information Systems personnel may have about the outsourcing firm and the new partnership between the two companies.

The last consideration is timing. It is imperative that you announce the decision to outsource at an optimum time. Since you have to assume this will be an announcement that will not be viewed as a positive event among the Information Systems organization, you will want to make the announcement at a time that will have the least amount of impact on the personnel and their productivity. I would suggest making the announcement on a Friday afternoon. This will allow everyone to think about the announcement over the weekend and reflect on the impact this will have on them personally. I would also suggest that, after the announcement on Friday, you arrange a meeting with the Information Systems personnel on the following Monday to start addressing their questions and concerns. For large companies where a single group meeting is not feasible due to various locations or a large number of people, you will want to have several of your managers hold meetings at their locations.

I would also suggest that the announcement not be held on a Friday prior to a 3-day holiday weekend. Needless to say, we all look forward to long weekends and this is not something that you would want to dampen the enthusiasm that a holiday weekend creates. One company made the announcement on the last work day prior to the Christmas holiday. The timing could not have been worse. In defense of the company, the announcement was necessary due to circumstances beyond their control. But regardless of the reason, the result was the same. It was a heck of a way to say "Merry Christmas." Once again, you should consult with your Human Resources representatives. They will be best qualified to determine when the appropriate time would be to inform the Information Systems personnel.

We have discussed the personnel that will be transitioning to the outsourcing firm and those that will remain as your company employees. There is a third category to consider: those whose services will no longer be required due to outsourcing. While there are many reasons that this could occur, such as consolidation of data centers, new systems implementation, and outsourcing training, the fact remains that positions will most likely be eliminated as a result of outsourcing. Typically, a company will also take this opportunity to replace individuals who are not meeting performance standards. Whether the details are provided at the time you make the announcement or not, employees will suspect that some will be transitioned, some will stay with your company, and some positions will be eliminated. This compounds the emotional trauma that accompanies an outsourcing decision.

Of course, this situation should be handled very carefully. Where possible, the employees should be offered a position elsewhere in your company. When this is not possible, most companies work with the individuals and a personnel placement agency to minimize the impact of job termination.

From a personnel standpoint, outsourcing can be a blow to their ego. Many times when we hear about a company outsourcing their Information Systems staff, it is automatically assumed that the Information Systems personnel were not able to do the job themselves. The truth of the matter is, when a company outsources it is usually to reduce Information Systems costs, control future growth, and take advantage of advanced technologies. Rarely are the current Information Systems personnel incapable of doing their job.

In contrast, it is usually found that the majority of personnel are transitioned to the outsourcing firm to continue what they have been doing. Be it a fair reputation or not, this is one of the dilemmas that the Chief Information Officer faces when the outsourcing decision is made. At times it is almost as though you should leave your ego and personal feelings at home and do what is best for the company, but we all know that is not always the easiest thing to do.

In summary, the line between a successful and unsuccessful transition is a very thin one. The methods for which you address personnel-related issues may very well determine how successful the total outsourcing partnership will be. Extreme care should be exercised when considering the effect that outsourcing will have on the Information Systems personnel. Keeping them informed of the outsourcing process and the exact status of the overall agreement from the time they are first told to the time the actual transition occurs is very important. The old saying, "the fear of the unknown," definitely applies. Throughout the process, put yourself in the shoes of the personnel who will be transitioned. Stop and think about how you would want to be treated if you were the one being transitioned. If all your actions are based with this thought in mind, you will minimize the number of issues that will arise with the Information Systems personnel. While the Information Systems personnel are professionals and you expect them to act accordingly, they are professionals with career goals, pride, and personal lives. Do not make the mistake of undermining the impact that outsourcing will have on each of your employees. As long as you focus on the positive aspects of outsourcing, project a confident and positive image throughout the outsourcing process, treat each person as an individual, and don't assume that everyone will agree with your viewpoints, you will minimize the personnel-related issues throughout the transitioning process.

9 Transitioning

After months of concentrated effort and countless hours of preparing your company for outsourcing, it is time to sign the contract. You know that the real beneficiaries of the agreement are your company, the Information Systems personnel, and the outsourcing firm, but once you have reached this point in the process you can't help but feel an overwhelming sense of accomplishment. No one can really begin to understand the trials and tribulations that the Chief Information Officer goes through during an outsourcing process. You have to be a businessman for the company, the personal friend of the transitioning Information Systems personnel, a strong negotiator with the outsourcing firm, and the one who has to keep it all together during the outsourcing process. Having done all this, you take great personal gratification in forming and negotiating the best outsourcing agreement possible. But once the contract is signed, and you have congratulated and rewarded your Outsourcing Team and celebrated your success with your new partner, it is time once again to go to work.

The next major task in the outsourcing journey is to ensure a smooth transition. The place to start is by promoting the newly formed partnership and advertising, both internally and externally, the strategic advantage that you and the outsourcing firm bring to each other. A well-planned and executed marketing campaign will accomplish several goals. First, your internal personnel will have a good understanding of what was done and why, and how it benefits your company. Second, it provides the information to your customers that your company is strategically focused on improving its services and relationships. This sends a clear message that your company is posturing itself for the future. The third significant advantage of the marketing campaign is that your competitors are now aware of a major and positive change in the company's strategic position. You've sent a strong message to them that by outsourcing you are strengthening your competitive advantage.

To ensure the smoothest transition possible, you will want to form a Transition Team. This team should consist of members from both your company and the outsourcing firm. The outsourcing firm will have its own Transitioning Team. This team's primary goal is to focus on the outsourcing firm and the transitioned personnel. This is all needed, but lacks the dedication and overall knowledge about your own company. By augmenting the outsourcing firm's Transition Team with members from your own company, you will have a team that is addressing the needs of both companies.

At the very least, the personnel on the team should consist of Human Resource representatives from both companies, the outsourcing firm's Account Manager, the Chief Information Officer, a senior representative from the nontransitioned Information Systems staff, and other representatives that both companies feel appropriate. This team's objectives would be to work with all Information Systems personnel, both transitioned and nontransitioned, to ensure all tasks in the transition plan are successfully completed. The Transition Team's primary objective is to ensure the transition takes place with minimum impact to your overall company. The whole reason for outsourcing should be based on improved benefits and possible cost savings. Therefore, you would not want to get started with a rocky transition.

Since this is the first time the non-Information Systems employees of your company will really be introduced to the performance capabilities of the outsourcing firm, it is important to have a smooth and seamless transition to form the proper levels of expectations and first impressions. By default, when a company outsources its Information Systems responsibilities, the rest of the company naturally assumes there will be a much improved Information Systems environment with the outsourcer. Further, this massive improvement is expected immediately. We all know that this is not the case. While you expect improvement, it is not realistic to think it can be accomplished overnight. In all likelihood it will take a period of months before the outsourcing firm can make a favorable impact on your company. Therefore, the transitioning team must make sure the proper expectations are established throughout the company.

As you start to think about the actual transitioning process, you should start documenting the tasks to be completed during this process. The best method that I have found for documenting these tasks is by, once again, utilizing project management software. This software will allow you to identify tasks and provide a means to keep track of the transitioning progress. A sample of the data that can be used is:

- Task name
- Start and stop dates
- Percent complete
- Preceding and succeeding tasks
- Responsible party for completing the task
- Deliverables
- Planned and actual costs
- Milestones
- Critical path

This information can be visually displayed so all appropriate parties can see the progress and remaining tasks to be completed at any point in time. Figure 9.1 is a typical project plan for transitioning to an outsourcing firm. This illustration contains tasks at a high level. Project schedules for your specific use should be as detailed as necessary to achieve the traceability and progress reporting required to achieve your objectives. Let's take a look at the tasks that would normally be included in all transitioning schedules to ensure a good understanding of their intent.

Maintenance Agreement

Earlier in the outsourcing process you have established the agreement between your company and the outsourcing firm as to who will be responsible for providing both hardware and software maintenance. For the maintenance responsibilities being transitioned to the outsourcing firm, you have to ensure you have the proper legal authority for the outsourcing firm to perform maintenance. Proper steps must be taken to ensure all appropriate maintenance agreements are either canceled or transferred to the outsourcing firm. This should all be accomplished before the actual transition.

Disaster Coverage

Assuming the outsourcing firm is taking responsibility for the majority of your Information Systems responsibilities, you have to ask yourself, "What will we do if, during the first few days of the transition, we have a significant disaster (e.g., a complete power outage) that affects the Information Systems controlled systems?" During the transition planning stage you should ensure that there is a clear understanding between your company and the outsourcer

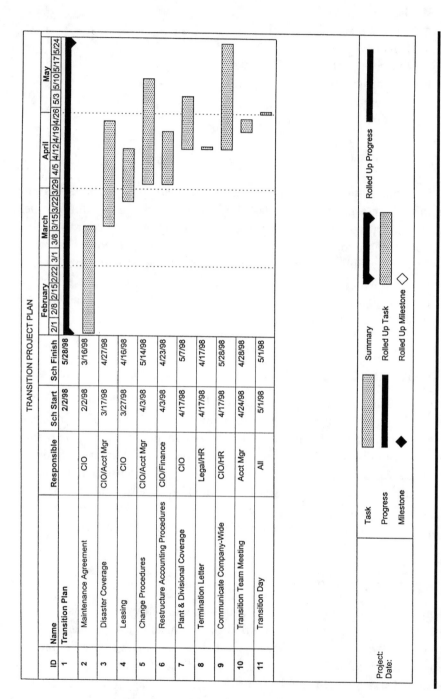

Figure 9.1   Transition Project Plan

as to what would be done in the event of a disaster, regardless of its magnitude, beginning the first hour of the transition.

Leasing

Assuming you currently have leasing agreements, you must ensure the outsourcing firm has the authority to use the leased equipment or software. As agreed upon in the negotiating phase, the responsible party (either the outsourcing firm or your company) should complete transactions to purchase the appropriate leases during the transition. Since purchasing a lease is a potentially large investment, this task will most likely be resolved between the appropriate parties prior to reaching this point in the process. As such, this exercise should be nothing more than executing the agreements that have already been established. In the event you have elected to retain the leased equipment, you should verify with the leasing company that the outsourcing firm personnel is authorized to use and maintain the equipment on your company's behalf.

Change Procedures

As a result of outsourcing, there will be existing procedures that will need to be revised. Potential examples of these procedures are: receiving Information Systems-related purchased materials; acquisition and distribution of supplies; and the method by which a problem is reported to the help desk. To ensure a smooth transition, you should have these procedures documented and established prior to the actual transition. The examples provided are just a few procedures that may be affected. You must ensure that all potential changes in procedures are identified and corrected prior to the transition.

Restructuring Accounting Procedures

Within your company there are specific accounting procedures that are used to track the cost of Information Systems. These procedures, such as intercompany charges and direct allocations, will most likely have to be revised to accommodate the methods for which you will track Information Systems-related costs after outsourcing. It may be a very simple process of continuing to track costs as you have in the past, or it may be a significant change requiring a great deal of effort and thought to develop an improved method for tracking costs and allocating the expenses throughout your company.

Included in this task should be the agreement between the outsourcing firm and your company stating how the outsourcing firm will invoice their services. There will be issues that you will have to address that are specific to outsourcing. Personal use tax, which is charged against consulting labor, is an example of the issues to be considered. You most likely have not had to deal with this in the past, but you now have to consider it as part of the accounting changes to be implemented. Again, it is important that these changes are defined and ready to be implemented upon transition. Discovering the changes required after the transition can be a very unpleasant experience. It is highly advisable to take time in the beginning of the process to clearly define the required changes to the accounting procedures. Failure to do so could result in additional costs that were not included in your analysis or budgets.

Plant and Divisional Coverage

Assuming your company has multiple locations and organizational divisions, it is essential that each location and separate organization be specifically addressed in the transition plan. Using the theme of "transitioning with minimal impact," you will want to ensure that each location is adequately informed and clearly understands how it is affected by the transition. Any processes or procedures that change as a result of the transition should be well communicated prior to the actual transition date.

Termination Letter

Assuming existing personnel are being transitioned to the outsourcing firm, there is usually a letter of termination that is required from your company. Generally, the employees are actually terminated from your company and hired by the outsourcing firm on the same day. Depending on your company policies for employee termination, you may have a requirement to send the termination letter to the employees within a fixed number of days prior to the actual termination. This should be reviewed closely with the Human Resources and legal departments to ensure that you conform with all guidelines and see that each transitioned employee receives the letter within the allotted time.

Communicate Company-Wide

As stated earlier, it is imperative that you communicate with the entire company and keep them informed of what is about to occur and why. This task is so essential to the success of the transition that it is advisable to place it in the transition plan to ensure that it is not overlooked. This is a time to overcommunicate. Assume nothing, and take every step possible to make sure the proper message is communicated to the company's employees.

The Outsourcing Firm Transition Team Meeting

As described above, the outsourcing firm will have its own Transition Team consisting of its Human Resources representatives and transitioning managers. This team will most likely make at least two visits to each of your facilities. The first is generally intended to be the official welcome and introduction to the outsourcing firm and the distribution of the benefits package. During this initial visit, the team will, of course, be prepared to answer questions and spend time with the transitioning personnel to ensure they are comfortable with the events that are about to take place. Their second visit will either be on the day of the transition or the previous day. This is when the transitioning personnel from your company are officially hired by the outsourcing firm. At this time, the employees sign up for the benefits of their choice and will no longer be on your company's payroll.

Transition Day

The actual transition day is recorded on the transition plan as a milestone. It is the day you have all been waiting for and working very hard to achieve. But the process does not end there. As you will find in Chapter 11, "Partnership Management," there is still much to be done. It is appropriate to advertise the transition day as a milestone event for the benefit of the company and the Information Systems personnel.

During the final days leading up to the transition and in the first few days following, it would be appropriate to escort the new outsourcing Account Manager around the various areas of the company and introduce him/her to the key personnel in your company. By this time, your entire company should be aware of the outsourcing event and should have received information on the importance of this strategic partnership and the benefits the outsourcing firm brings to your company. Of course there will be mixed emotions regarding this partnership. For the most part you will find that if the outsourcing event was properly promoted and advertised, the majority of employees will be supportive and eager to work with the outsourcing firm. One of the biggest tasks for the Account Manager is to build a positive rapport with managers and employees throughout the company. As we all know, this positive rapport is based on respect and is not something that can be delegated. It must be earned. Provided you have done an adequate job of promoting the outsourcing partnership, the Account Manager will have a good foundation to start this crucial task.

In summary, the transition to the outsourcing firm is a critical event that must be handled properly. A smooth transition can literally make a difference between a successful partnership and a rocky partnership. Since transition day will be the first day many non-Information Systems personnel encounter the outsourcing firm, it is imperative that you and the outsourcing firm make a great first impression. While the Chief Information Officer and the outsourcing firm's Account Manager will be dealing with contract issues such as maintenance and leasing contracts during the transition, your success will be largely based on how well the personnel-related tasks are handled. The personnel-related tasks include those associated with the Information Systems personnel being transitioned, the Information Systems personnel staying with your company, the Information Systems personnel whose positions are being eliminated, and all the non-Information Systems personnel throughout your company. As long as you establish realistic expectations, remember that you are dealing with people, and treat them in a fair and professional manner, you will find that the transition will go as smoothly as expected.

10 When To Use Consultants

Regardless of the task, it is common for companies to utilize the assistance of industry consultants. There are two primary reasons for using consultants — first, to assist in managing staffing requirements; second, to take advantage of current industry experience and knowledge that may be lacking in your organization. When considering outsourcing, it is appropriate to assume that you will need assistance from a consulting firm which specializes in outsourcing. Making the decision as to whether or not to outsource your Information Systems responsibilities is a major process. The decision has the potential for significant impact on both your organization and its personnel. It is something that should not be taken lightly nor should you assume that your current organization has the knowledge base necessary to make an informed decision. As a result, it is highly advisable to enlist a consultant to assist you throughout the process.

As we all know, selecting a consulting firm is not easy. There are many consulting firms with excellent references that can provide the services you need. The problem is determining which one can provide the most benefit at a reasonable cost. Since Information Systems outsourcing is a process that many organizations have never been involved with, it is difficult to know what questions to ask or even to know where to start looking for the right consulting firm for outsourcing. To assist in the process of determining which consulting firm is best for your company, the following are a few suggestions to consider:

1. Length of time involved in outsourcing
2. Outsourcing firm affiliation

3. Success rate
4. References
5. Current client base
6. Amount of value directly contributed to process
7. Methodology used

Considering these areas when selecting an outsourcing firm will result in a good understanding of the firm's experience; however, there may be other considerations that you may want to evaluate. You will need to take a closer look at each of the above considerations to further highlight the importance of each category.

Length of Time Involved in Outsourcing

Due to large demand and strong economic growth, there are numerous consulting firms today that advertise as providing Information Systems outsourcing assistance. While many of the outsourcing consulting firms are well established and have been in existence for some time, there are others who are relative newcomers to the industry. Just because a consulting firm may be relatively new does not necessarily mean that it cannot provide value-added consulting services for you. This is as important for you to remember as the fact that because a consulting firm has been around for many years, and has many professionals providing outsourcing consulting services, does not guarantee you a successful consulting engagement.

The most important aspect of selecting a consulting firm is getting to know the actual consultant who will be assigned to your account and being comfortable with his/her credentials and personality. You certainly do not want someone who has never successfully led an outsourcing process nor would you want someone who has never been involved in the outsourcing process for multiple companies. Just as important as professional qualifications is the consultant's personality. You can have the best-qualified person assigned to your account, but if your personalities do not mesh, the risk of completing a successful consulting engagement is much higher.

Outsourcing Firm Affiliation

When selecting a consulting firm, it is important to understand the relationship the consulting firm may have with various outsourcing firms. To ensure that you will be represented by a truly nonbiased consulting firm, it is important to ensure that the consulting firm has no current business partnerships or business alliances with specific outsourcing firms. Instead, you should be looking for a consulting firm that has had experience with multiple outsourcing firms. In this way, the potential for receiving the best advice is much higher.

This does not imply that the consulting firms should not have professional business contacts with personnel at specific outsourcing firms. In fact, the consultant specializing in Information Systems outsourcing will have contacts within the more established outsourcing organizations through working with various outsourcing firms. This too can be a measure of how qualified a particular consultant is for your company. The number of contacts a consultant has with multiple outsourcing firms is an indication of their acceptance and experience within the industry.

You should consider the consulting firm's responsibility as advisory only. The ultimate decision of which outsourcing firm to select has to come from within your organization. The consulting firm should provide recommendations for advantages and disadvantages of each alternative, but the final decision has to be yours. As a result, you do not want to engage a consulting firm that stands to gain financially from a decision of using one outsourcing firm over another.

Success Rate

Something you rarely see or hear about is the fact that not all companies that start the outsourcing process complete the project with an outsourcing agreement. As mentioned in earlier chapters, every Chief Information Officer should evaluate the feasibility of outsourcing the Information Systems organization. The outsourcing process does not necessarily result in an outsourcing agreement. The reason for this decision varies from company to company. Many times it is found that the cost of outsourcing exceeds the benefit. Another reason is that the consulting firm utilized did not provide good advice or was not able to demonstrate the necessary qualifications required for such an undertaking.

A good question to ask potential consulting firms would be for the number of companies to whom they proposed their outsourcing consulting services, but were not selected. Stated another way, "What is their ratio of successful versus unsuccessful accounts?" Beware of the consulting firm that tells you they have never had a failed account or an account where the final results were less than expected. No one wins 100% of the time. Realistic expectations would be something less than 100%. A good consulting firm, however, will win a large majority of the business it seeks. A general rule of thumb is that highly successful consulting firms win approximately 80% of the business they target.

You should also consider the number of clients that have signed with a consulting firm and are considered to be a referenceable account. While this may be difficult to determine, it is definitely a question worth asking. Of the accounts that the consulting firm has been working with over the past two to three years, how many are they willing to give you as a referenceable account? This again is a subjective measure, but would be in your best interest to pursue. There are bound to be times when a customer is not completely satisfied with a specific consulting service, the fault cannot be directly attributed to the consulting firm. As a result, it is common to find that something less than 100% of clients are referenceable. This measure, however, should be in the high 90th percentile for a consulting firm that delivers high-quality services.

References

Once you have found a consulting firm qualified to address your specific needs, it is always advisable to ask for several references. It is a well-known fact that many professionals feel that checking references is a waste of time. However, it is still a viable step in the process when selecting a consulting firm. Many professionals ask, "Why check references when you know the references that are given will be positive ones?" The answer is simple. When working with clients in complicated outsourcing projects, companies quickly find the true value that the consulting firm can provide to their organization. Information Systems consulting can be done with several different approaches and methodologies. Checking references will provide insight on how the consulting firm reacts to certain situations and the overall value the consulting firm brought to the outsourcing process.

I have never seen a company, after going through a major outsourcing project, that said they wouldn't do it differently if they did it over again. This is another reason why you would want to follow up with references. This provides you with a good opportunity to discuss the outsourcing process with these references and ask what they would do differently, and why. This affords you the ability to evaluate the potential consulting firm and learn more about the outsourcing process in general — again, by learning from others' mistakes.

When checking the references of outsourcing firms, the following are some areas to consider and potential questions you may want to ask:

- Did the consulting firm deliver the services as promised?
- Was the estimated cost of the agreement exceeded during the project?
- Did the primary consultant assigned to the project require additional assistance? If so, what type of assistance was required and was the assistance provided through his/her company or a third-party consulting firm?
- Do you feel that having the consulting firm working with you resulted in a better agreement with the outsourcing firm?
- Was the consulting firm helpful in establishing your expectations for the outsourcing process?
- Did the consulting firm provide additional information that assisted you in defining the overall scope of the outsourcing agreement?
- What methods did the consulting firm use to assist in the problem-solving process?
- Did the consulting firm assist you in determining what part of the Information Systems organization should be outsourced? If so, how was this done?
- If you were going through the outsourcing process again, would you use the same consulting firm, and why?
- Knowing what you know today about the outsourcing process, what would you do differently if you were going to repeat the process?
- Did the consulting firm assist you in negotiating the contract with the outsourcing firm? If so, what role did the consulting firm assume, and what value did they bring to the negotiation process?
- Do you feel the consulting firm was aware of the potential outsourcing firms that would best fit their needs?
- How did the consulting firm convince you that their recommendations were based on proven experience?
- Did the same personnel work with you from start to finish? If not, why?
- Do you feel that the consulting firm utilized current methodologies and technologies to assist you during the outsourcing process? If so, what were they?

The above questions are just samples of the kind of information that would be pertinent to objectively evaluate one consulting firm over another. The actual questions you will need to ask depend upon your environment and specific needs. Regardless of the questions asked, they should be consistent with each reference you check, so you will have a good basis for comparing companies.

When talking with a reference provided by the consulting firm, you should ask for other companies that they are aware of that use the same consulting firm. This may give you an opportunity to follow up with companies that have used the consulting firm but that were not given to you as a reference. At times, this can be a valuable exercise and provide an opportunity to gather information that may otherwise not be available to you.

Checking references is highly recommended. Done properly it is an excellent way to obtain valuable information about a consulting firm and the overall value they bring to the process. It is also an excellent way to avoid problems and issues that have already been addressed by other companies. Checking references can provide you with a better feeling about the long-range partnership you are about to establish with a consulting firm.

Current Client Base

When selecting a consulting firm, it is appropriate to think about how current the consulting firm's experience is. As we all know, Information Technology changes rapidly, so it is essential that you determine if the consulting firm has kept pace. Reviewing its current client base and understanding the scope of the consulting firm's involvement with its clients will provide you with a better grasp of the consulting firm's involvement and understanding of the outsourcing process. It would also be appropriate to include the current client base in the process of checking references. Doing so will give you a good comparison of how the consulting firm has performed in the past and how they are performing today.

The Amount of Value Directly Contributed to the Process

One of the main reasons companies seek the assistance of consulting firms during the outsourcing process is to ensure that they will be receiving value-added services that exceed their current abilities. As a result, it is appropriate to evaluate the amount of value-added service that a consulting firm has contributed to previous customers. During the selection process for a consulting firm, you should question the consulting firm's references in regard to the amount that the consulting firm has contributed to the overall process. This contribution should be in monetary as well as intangible benefits. Examples of intangible benefits are:

- The education that the consulting firm brings to your organization
- The knowledge exchange that naturally occurs during a consulting effort
- Advice on which outsourcing firms to pursue
- Setting the proper expectations within your company
- Assistance in evaluating the scope of the outsourcing project
- Providing recommendations on whether or not to include selected Information Systems personnel as part of the outsourcing agreement

There are many other intangible benefits that your company could realize. It is advisable, and many companies do this, to maintain a record of the estimated value contributed as a result of intangible benefits. In doing so, you will understand the total value a consulting firm brings to your company.

Tangible contributions are primarily centered around the amount of money the consulting firm has saved you as a result of its involvement in the process. When considering the value a consulting firm would bring your company, it is realistic to expect that the consulting firm would, at a minimum, save your company enough money to offset the cost of engaging it. This would be demonstrated during the contract negotiation phase of the outsourcing process and during the time you are developing the request for proposal.

If approached properly, it is fairly easy to identify the specific advice and negotiation techniques that the consulting firm brings to the process that will result in overall cost savings, or avoidance, for your company. If you are unable to identify these savings, I would suggest you are not getting the value from your consulting firm that you are paying for and deserve.

Methodology Used

When speaking with any consulting firm, it will advertise the methodologies that it employs during the outsourcing process. As with anything else, some methodologies are better than others. The important thing is to understand the methodology the consulting firm utilizes and make sure you agree with it. Consulting firms spend a great deal of time instructing and teaching their consultants to conduct business in a certain manner. If you decide, after you have contracted with a consulting firm, that you do not agree with their methodologies, it can be difficult to change the way the consulting firm approaches the outsourcing process for your company. As a result, you should closely consider and understand the methodologies that each consulting firm uses before you make your final decision about which consulting firm to use.

This does not mean you have to agree with every word or every step in the methodology being utilized. Any good consulting firm will be flexible to a point. So long as you agree with the concepts and general approach to the consulting firm's methodologies, the detailed steps and actions can be modified to accommodate your specific requirements and environment.

One word of caution when evaluating the methodologies: there are consulting firms that utilize methodologies that require moving consulting personnel in and out of an account. It has been my experience that this is not the best approach. While it is well understood that no one can be a specialist in every area, there should always be one person who is the single point of contact and has the overall responsibility for the success of the consulting engagement. This person should be the same person throughout the outsourcing process.

It should also be understood that this single point of contact within the consulting firm is the person who schedules other consultants with professional specialties as, and if, needed. Regardless of the circumstances, no company can guarantee that a specific person will be the single point of contact. As a result, the consulting agreement should be structured so that the consulting firm will take all measures, to the best of its abilities, to ensure that the person you selected to be the lead consultant will be the single point of contact throughout the consulting agreement. You should also state in the contract that in the event the primary consulting individual leaves the consulting firm or is reassigned for any reason, that you will have the right to cancel the contract, or the right to interview and select his/her replacement.

Following these guidelines will help you determine the best consulting firm to assist you during your outsourcing process. Again, it is strongly advisable to always use a third-party consulting firm that specializes in working with outsourcing firms. Regardless of the amount of research you do, the bottom line in selecting a consulting firm usually ends up being a "gut feel." There are many excellent companies today that provide consulting services for outsourcing. As a result, it is very common for companies to go through a very detailed selection process and still have two or three companies they feel are very qualified and price competitive. As such, the final decision is one of emotion and a leap of faith.

However, this is an exercise that should not be taken lightly. Selecting the wrong consulting firm has the potential of costing you hundreds of thousands of dollars. This cost comes from the consulting firm's fees as well as its failure to provide savings and cost avoidance. On the other hand, selecting the right consulting firm should most definitely result in significant savings and a process that will be both professionally rewarding and beneficial for all parties.

11 Partnership Management

A partnership is like a marriage: both parties must have a commitment to make a consistent, strong effort to ensure that they are doing all they possibly can to make the marriage work. Both your company and the outsourcing firm should have entered into the partnership with the full understanding that it will be a give-and-take relationship. The fact that both companies have signed a contract obviously indicates that both are confident it will be a profitable and/or cost-saving undertaking. They should also understand that this will only occur if both companies work together to resolve all issues that come up during the term of the contract. Having reached the point where the contract has been signed and the transition completed, the outsourcing firm's Account Manager and your Chief Information Officer, assuming the Chief Information Officer is the individual the Account Manager will be reporting to, must have the utmost confidence in each other to do the job that is required. Only then can you expect a successful partnership.

While you should have the greatest respect for your new business partner, you should also ensure that the proper performance measurements are established and monitored so you can achieve the desired results as promised throughout the outsourcing process. Meaningful performance measures for the Information Technology profession have always been difficult to define, measure, and quantify. But this should not be an excuse for not developing the proper performance measures for you and the outsourcing firm's Account Manager to use as a guideline for establishing goals, identifying potential problem areas, and recognizing achievements. There are many different types of performance measures that can be used to achieve this objective. The main point is to remember that there are only four meaningful performance indicators that are truly useful in improving your relationship with the outsourcing firm. The four performance indicators are measures that track changes and trends in:

1. Improved quality
2. Reduced lead time
3. Improvement in the level of service
4. Reduced costs

All other measures tend to be meaningless in their overall contribution to the big picture.

Listed below are a few performance measures that may be used for your specific requirements. These are just suggestions and should not be used if they cannot be tied back to one of the four performance indicators listed above. The performance measures are:

- Function point analysis
- CPU availability
- CPU response time
- Terminal response time
- Network response time
- Initial call close rate
- Network availability
- Average time to respond to a problem
- Average time required to correct a problem
- Number of defects per 100 lines of code
- Average personnel turnover rate
- Average absenteeism rate
- Information Systems costs stated as a percentage of sales
- Number and percent of job reruns due to operator error

Regardless of the performance measures used, you should ensure the outsourcing firm is meeting the objectives as defined and agreed upon during the negotiations process. Another means for measurement would be the Service Level Agreement (SLA) defined in Chapter 4. The Service Level Agreement is the contractual performance measure that the outsourcing firm needs to meet. At the very least, the outsourcing firm must adhere to the performance measures established in the Service Level Agreement. Failure to do so will result in a breach of contract from which neither the outsourcing firm nor your company would benefit.

Since an outsourcing agreement covers multiple years, it is quite conceivable that new performance measurement tools and techniques will become available over the length of the agreement. Both the outsourcing firm's Account Manager and your Chief Information Officer should be aware of new measures and take advantage of them whenever possible. After all, you want the outsourcing partnership to work as much as they do, and both companies want to do the best job possible. Therefore, as technology advances, both companies should take advantage of every opportunity to improve Information Technology services.

An added benefit of maintaining good performance measures is that they provide good quantitative data with which to compare your initial assessment of expected savings with what is actually taking place. Like everything else, you can learn from this experience and apply the knowledge in future business dealings.

Another aspect of partnership management is the care and nurturing of your supplier relationships. Prior to outsourcing, you dealt strictly with your suppliers without any other influencing factors. After outsourcing, you may or may not be dealing with the same suppliers, but now you have the outsourcing firm as the driving force for identifying the requirements and specifications for any new hardware, software, or professional service purchases. As we all know, positive supplier/customer relationships are important, and you would not want to do anything to bruise these relationships unless it was absolutely necessary.

Depending on which outsourcing firm you have contracted with, they may be a supplier from which you can acquire your hardware and software. In this case, the outsourcing firm can provide price quotes (on a predetermined basis, e.g., semiannually) and be considered a source of supply. Care should be taken to ensure that, in the event your outsourcing firm can fill your hardware and software procurement needs, they are not necessarily an automatic win. It is important that your other suppliers understand this. It is common for suppliers to assume that once a company outsources, they will no longer be able to compete for future business. By communicating to the suppliers that the supplier/customer relationship will still be intact, you will be able to retain them as sources of supply. This will ensure that the outsourcing firm will stay competitive with pricing or take the chance of losing business.

In order to ensure competitive rates, you will want to compete your new business and, on occasion, ensure that other suppliers are awarded a portion of the business. In the event that the outsourcing firm is always the lowest bidder, the other suppliers may eventually not care to provide a price quote and you will eventually lose them as a competitor of the outsourcing firm. This is not to say that you should avoid going to the outsourcing firm for new purchases. Be aware if you do purchase from the outsourcing firm, they could increase prices over time to the point where they will no longer be competitive. It would benefit you and your company to ensure that the prices are competed on occasion to ensure that you are getting the best possible value for the money spent.

In addition to price, there is also value-added in availability. In some cases, one supplier may be the low bidder, but the items needed might not be available immediately and maybe you cannot wait. An example of this would be parts for a network file server that is in a "production down" status. Assuming the server is a mission-essential component of your network, you must get the server back into production as quickly as possible. In this case, you are willing to pay an additional price for the fast turnaround of replacement components. As with anything else, just use good common sense in supplier/customer relationships. Put yourself in their shoes and treat the suppliers in a fair, professional manner.

You have to expect the supplier/customer relationship to be different after outsourcing. Most suppliers view outsourcing firms as major competitors extremely difficult to compete with. But once again, you have a business to run and cannot afford to put all your eggs in one basket without expecting problems in the future. You want to maintain positive supplier/customer relationships for cases in which the outsourcing firm may not be able to deliver the required materials or services.

Another key element in partnership management is establishing the proper expectations for both your company and the outsourcing firm. To assume that the outsourcing firm will continue at the same level of performance and efficiency that your Information Systems organization has realized in the past is a bad assumption. If this were the case, you would have a hard time justifying outsourcing. There would be no value-added in outsourcing if you would be getting the same level of service and performance that you would get without it. The proper expectations should be established which identify the improvement that the outsourcing firm will bring. This improvement will not be realized immediately; it will take months before the real benefits start to be noticeable.

By establishing the performance measures, you will have the information you need to establish the proper expectations across the company. Clear performance measures will allow the outsourcing firm to know what is expected. It will also place you in a position to inform the remainder of your company's employees of the goals and objectives that both the outsourcing firm and your company have agreed upon. This sets the expectations at a manageable level and provides a set of achievable objectives. Once the proper expectations are established, it will be up to the outsourcing firm and your senior management to ensure that the objectives are met.

Outsourcing your Information Systems duties does not relieve your company of responsibilities. As a Chief Information Officer, you should still be held accountable for the success of the systems environment and the overall value it brings to the company. To ensure success, you will have to constantly work with the outsourcing account team and refine the partnership as it matures. If you have done your job correctly throughout the outsourcing process, you will be pleased with the overall decisions that you have made and the effects of the decisions. You will also have a rock solid contract that clearly specifies what responsibilities the outsourcing firm has and the level at which it should perform its tasks. The outsourcing firm will know that it is in their best interest to refine and improve the relationship. All outsourcing firms rely heavily on existing customers' word-of-mouth advertising. As a result, it is of utmost importance for them to ensure a good relationship and a successful partnership with your company.

There will always be surprises as you continue your journey with the outsourcing firm. As you have found, it is impossible to think of everything during the outsourcing process. As events arise that are not clearly specified in the contract, both your company and the outsourcing firm should work closely to resolve the issues and not get caught up in contract "scope creep." Scope creep is defined as small tasks that are continually added to the contract after it is signed. As the contract matures, more and more out-of-scope conditions will be added to the overall value of the contract. This is a no-win situation for both the outsourcing firm and your company.

A well-written contract will prevent disputes regarding out-of-scope conditions. The scope of work should be clearly stated in the contract, and both the outsourcing firm and your company should be flexible in the daily execution of the contractual agreements. This will be a give-and-take partnership. Scope of work should only become an issue for major changes in business (e.g., purchase or sale of a manufacturing plant, total replacement of systems not included in the original contract, etc.). Once the rumor starts that "every time you turn around, the outsourcing firm is complaining about out-of-scope tasks" you will lose control of the overall perception of the value the outsourcing firm brings to your company. This is why it is so essential to take time during the contracting and negotiating process to ensure that the majority of scope issues are addressed and that there is enough flexibility, for both companies, to allow for smaller business changes throughout the contract term.

Throughout this text, we have reviewed the methods and procedures for successfully outsourcing all or part of your Information Systems organization. To illustrate the importance and absolute critical aspect of the outsourcing process, Appendix E provides a look at a case study of a company that successfully completed the initial outsourcing process but failed to effectively manage their partnership with the outsourcing firm.

12 Summary

Outsourcing Information Systems responsibilities has become a viable business option for many companies. Throughout this text, we have looked at the process a company would normally go through to determine whether or not to outsource. As we have learned, outsourcing isn't always the right decision. However, it is impossible to make that decision without going through the process of evaluating its feasibility for your specific company. While the result of this evaluation may be a decision to *not* outsource, you and your Outsourcing Team will identify opportunities for improvement as a result of conducting the outsourcing process.

The opportunities for improvement will vary by company, but without exception there will be some areas identified for improvement. Just because the outsourcing evaluation focused on Information Systems does not mean that areas for improvement would be found only in the Information Systems organization. Done properly, the outsourcing process encompasses all the major business processes your company is currently using. When talking with outsourcing firms, it is highly likely that they will be identifying potential areas for improvement in areas other than Information Systems. The recommended areas for improvement would normally be documented in the outsourcing firm's proposal. As a result, you and your Outsourcing Team will have the information needed to begin an improvement effort within your company that may or may not include the outsourcing firm.

The bottom line to answering the question, "Why would a company want to outsource?," is the simple answer, "You might not!" This absolutely depends upon your specific circumstances and the overall business environment within which you are currently operating. The future strategic initiatives of your company also play a major role in deciding whether or not to outsource. If your current Information Systems staff does not have the knowledge to take your company to a higher level of technology, or you feel the amount of money that's spent each year is going into a non-value-added function, then it is definitely a good idea to assess the feasibility of outsourcing. Regardless of your decision, you will not be sorry that you have taken the time to evaluate the possibilities of outsourcing for your company.

With today's highly competitive marketplace, companies are searching for everything possible to help them realize a competitive advantage. Information Systems outsourcing can potentially be a significant driver in providing the competitive edge in your company. In manufacturing, the goal has always been to have the right material at the right place at the right time. Where feasible, just-in-time material flow methodologies have been implemented to reduce the costs of manufacturing. This concept has now extended throughout the entire supplier and customer base and has formed the supply chain management methodologies that are currently being implemented in manufacturing companies. Information Systems outsourcing can strengthen the supply chain management initiatives by providing the appropriate technology for your company, as well as for other companies within your supply chain, at the time they are needed. Outsourcing also gives your company competitive leverage to assist your customers and suppliers in implementing technologies in their own companies. Without having the outsourcing firm's resources available to you, this may not be possible.

The retail industry depends on having consumer goods where needed and when needed. By working with the outsourcing firms, many companies in the retail industry are able to take advantage of the outsourcing firm's global communications infrastructure to transact business with their supplier and distribution networks, thus reducing the amount of supplier lead time and on-hand material that must be maintained.

In the banking industry the difference between a profitable and nonprofitable organization may very well depend upon the speed and accuracy with which your company is able to transact business. The larger outsourcing firms today have very elaborate, global infrastructures that allow the banking industry to communicate with anybody in the world at anytime, thus providing a means to transfer funds within seconds, regardless of location, throughout the world.

While the above examples represent only three industries, outsourcing can be a viable option for all industries. Regardless of the industry, Information Systems outsourcing has had, and continues to have, a profound positive impact on business in general. Allowing companies to focus on their core efficiencies and not have to worry about maintaining a technical staff to remain competitive can definitely, under the right circumstances, increase a company's competitive advantage.

We have also looked at how best to develop an outsourcing strategy. The outsourcing strategy is critical to the overall success of the outsourcing effort. As with any business venture, a flawed strategy could result in disaster. Once you have decided you are going to look at the feasibility of outsourcing, the reasons you are undertaking the task and the process by which you will evaluate the feasibility are very important. Having a clear understanding of these two areas will help to ensure that the proper questions are being asked of your organization, as well as the potential outsourcing firms.

This does not mean that, once you start the outsourcing process and find that your strategy is something less than desired, you cannot change your strategy. If this is the case, your strategy should be modified early in the process to ensure the least impact on the overall project. To ensure a good start, take the time to build an outsourcing strategy that will ensure a fair and professional evaluation and decisions based on business-related facts.

We have also discussed the value of creating partnerships required when outsourcing. It is absolutely essential that a rock solid partnership be developed with the outsourcing firm. Without this partnership, the decision to outsource may only end up being a very bad business decision. Many companies have found that outsourcing takes a great deal of work, not only in the initial steps but after the contract is signed. Good business partnerships are like long friendships: they do not happen overnight but have to be built over a long period of time. When developing these business partnerships, it is essential to be straightforward and open with your outsourcing firm. You should expect nothing less in return. Building a partnership is definitely a two-way street. Without the give-and-take approach, it will be extremely difficult for both companies to develop a long-term business partner.

We have also discussed the feasibility and importance of developing requests for proposals. Many individuals feel that request for proposals are an exercise of little value. When it comes to selecting an Information Systems outsourcing firm, I strongly disagree with this. When considering outsourcing, there is so much that has to be reviewed and discussed that it is impossible to adequately compare one outsourcing firm to another without having some way of normalizing the information being received from each outsourcing firm. The request for proposal provides you an opportunity to establish the level of expectations and requirements for each of the potential outsourcing firms to respond. Without this level of common understanding across the outsourcing firms, it would be impossible to compare apples to apples when reviewing the various proposals from outsourcing firms.

Developing a request for proposal is not, by any means, a trivial task. It takes a lot of time, dedication, and internal negotiation to establish a good request for proposal that you and your company will feel comfortable presenting to the outsourcing firms. The request for proposal also gives you an opportunity to educate the potential outsourcing firms in the history of your company and the current status and long-range goals of your Information Systems environment. This too will give you the advantage of having potential outsourcing firms quote on a long-term business agreement and having the proper inter-company knowledge required to achieve a realistic and feasible proposal from your outsourcing firms.

After receiving the proposals, you should evaluate them based on criteria that have been well defined in advance. The proposal evaluation process can be enjoyable. After many weeks and months of time dedicated to developing the request for proposal, it is always nice to see the level of understanding and thoroughness that an outsourcing firm has about your company. The proposals will be a major factor in deciding whether or not you will outsource. If the final decision is to outsource, the proposals will be major contributors in determining the outsourcing firm of choice.

A great deal of care and consideration should be given to the methods that will be employed to evaluate the proposals. It is not feasible to think that this evaluation can be done through first impressions or human instincts. There are just too many factors to consider to think that the evaluation can be done quickly and fairly unless you have the proper tools and methods defined to assist in the process. Rather, this is the time to draw upon your years of decision analysis experience and deploy the best tools possible to assist in the decision process. Doing so will assist in the evaluation of the proposals, as well as give you sound information on which to base your decisions to eliminate candidates who did not fare well during your review. This will also strengthen your position on why you would like to select a specific candidate. A proper and thorough job with the proposal evaluation provides you with excellent information that will be required later in the internal approval process.

Having completed the proposal evaluation and selected the outsourcing firm that best meets your needs, the next area of focus is to develop the contract. As an obviously critical document, the contract must survive the test of time. Since outsourcing agreements are generally 5 to 10 years in duration, it is essential that the contract be very specific in as many areas as possible. It is also essential to ensure as much flexibility as possible. We all know that it is impossible to define absolutely everything that might occur over the next 10 years. As a result, both you and the outsourcing firm must have the flexibility to continue to build the relationship between the two companies without entering into a breach of contract condition. This has to be carefully documented in the contract to allow both companies the flexibility required. However, the flexibility cannot overshadow the need to be specific about what's expected of the outsourcing firm. The best way to address your expectations is through performance measures that can be documented in the contract. These performance measures are critical to ensuring that the outsourcing company is meeting your expectations now and in the future.

An outsourcing contract contains many clauses that help you reduce your risk and ensure that the outsourcing company delivers the products and services as promised. While there are many similarities between an outsourcing contract and other service-related contracts, due to the length of time involved and the nature of the services being provided in an outsourcing agreement, there are specific clauses that would be appropriate for an outsourcing contract that would not be appropriate for other service-related contracts. Regardless of your level of experience dealing with contracts, this is an area in which you should definitely seek third-party assistance. Having legal counsel that specializes in Information Systems outsourcing agreements helps ensure that you are not missing something that would not be discovered until months or years after the contract effective date.

While you should view the contract as a document to assist your company in reducing your risk, you should also view it as a means for the outsourcing firm to do the same. The outsourcing firm needs to reduce its risk for long-term partnerships as well. It too will be viewing the contract as an absolute means to accomplish this goal. As a result, it would be appropriate for the outsourcing firm to insist upon documenting your company's obligations in the contract.

As with any step of the Outsourcing Model, illustrated in Figure 1.1, the contracting phase of the Information Systems outsourcing process should be clearly defined and given the proper time to do an effective job. Developing an outsourcing contract is not the time to cut corners to save time. Doing so will increase your overall risk and increase the opportunities for failure.

During the same time you're developing the contract with the outsourcing firm, you will also be negotiating the overall agreement. This is another area in which it would be appropriate to seek third-party assistance. Negotiating an outsourcing agreement is far different than any other type of negotiation. As a result, to do an effective job requires specialized skills that one normally would not find within his/her company. It can be a great value to seek legal counsel and/or a consultant who specializes in Information Systems outsourcing. While this may prolong the overall process, it will be well worth the initial time invested.

There are many ways to negotiate an outsourcing agreement. It is essential that your Outsourcing Team clearly develop a negotiating strategy before starting the process. Doing so will assist you in achieving an agreement that will stand the test of time and leave your company and the outsourcing firm feeling you have achieved an overall good agreement.

One would think that after selecting an outsourcing firm and negotiating an agreement the hard work of initializing an outsource agreement would be finished. This is not the case. You still have the personnel issue to deal with. Assuming your agreement will include transitioning personnel to the outsourcing firm, the most stressful part of the outsourcing process is yet to come. Many Information Systems professionals view the outsourcing activity as an indication that the Information Systems organization has failed their company. This is rarely the case. Normally, outsourcing agreements are reached because of business conditions, not because the Information Systems organization failed to address its company's needs. This is easy to say, but difficult to sell. Just ask any Information Systems professional who has been part of an outsourcing transition process. They will tell you that their initial feelings were one of surprise and "Why me?" As discussed in the text, the SARA (Surprise, Anger, Reconciliation, and Acceptance) model clearly defines the emotional stages you can expect from your Information Systems professionals. Without exception, everyone will go through, with varying degrees of intensity, the various steps of the SARA model.

Something else you can expect is to be totally surprised yourself in regard to how some of your professionals will react to the news. You can count on all of your staff to be surprised, assuming that the word has not leaked prior to your announcement. What you may not count on is the reaction from a select few individuals. Often, those individuals you think would take the news lightly will be the hardest hit by the information. On the other hand, those you think might react strongly are often the easiest to deal with. Regardless, it is always difficult to go through this part of the process.

No one likes to upset someone else. The important thing is to be prepared when you announce the outsourcing agreement and keep your personnel well informed of the status of the transition. It is often said that the biggest fear of change is caused by lack of information. The same can be said for outsourcing transition personnel. You will find that the more information you can give the Information Systems personnel, the faster you will gain their acceptance. There will be a time for them to adjust to the idea, as described in the discussion about the SARA model, but the faster you can get the information to the employees, the faster they will reach the acceptance stage of the process.

The bottom line with transitioning personnel is to keep them as informed as possible, be patient, and put yourself in their shoes. You should handle each question and concern from each of the employees as though it is the most important question of his/her career, because in the employee's eyes, it may very well be.

Once you decide to go through an outsourcing process, it is highly advisable to enlist the assistance of an industry specialist. This specialist, or consultant, should be part of the entire process. This involvement should be from when you first thought you might want to outsource until after the agreement has been signed and the personnel have been transitioned. Again, you are investing a great deal of money and time in outsourcing. The industry consultants can help to assure that you are getting the most value for your investment. Failure to use a good consultant could potentially cause you to miss many things in the outsourcing process and end up with an agreement with an outsourcing firm that is far less than you expected. With the proper consultant on your team, the incremental cost for having a consultant can be far outweighed by the amount of savings and risk reduction that the consultant should be able to provide.

Strong consideration should be given to which consulting firm to utilize. Take time to evaluate different consulting firms. Doing so will help to ensure that the consultant you select is the best fit for your company and your long-range goals. Anything less could be detrimental to your company.

Once the contract has been signed and the personnel have been transitioned, it is time to turn your attention to developing the partnership with your selected outsourcing firm. This is accomplished by managing the partnership to ensure the relationship stays on track within the guidelines of the contract. Your goal should be to stay on top of the partnership until it matures into a true business partnership from which both companies can enjoy the benefits.

Assuming that the partnership will come naturally between the two companies is a bad assumption. There have been many examples, similar to the case history contained herein, of companies that have not paid enough attention to developing the partnership. As a result, many Information Systems outsourcing ventures have failed. By paying attention to the business of outsourcing and partnership development you can avoid these pitfalls and ensure that your relationship with the outsourcing firm remains strong and strengthens over time.

Outsourcing has become a much talked-about topic throughout industry. What was once an option only for large companies has now become a viable option for most companies. Without question, outsourcing is not for everyone. It is up to you and your company to evaluate the feasibility of outsourcing and determine if it is a feasible business venture for your company. As stated earlier, the outsourcing process is one that I highly recommend each company go through. While the end result may be a decision not to outsource, I can guarantee that as a result of going through the process, your company will identify opportunities you might have never realized otherwise. You have to weigh the benefits, risks, advantages, and disadvantages for your specific company in order to assess the applicability of outsourcing for your needs. Anyone who has gone through the outsourcing process has gained a much better appreciation for the amount of work it takes to successfully create a partnership that is beneficial for all parties. The individuals involved in the outsourcing process will also gain a great deal of professional experience.

If your actions are based on good sound business reasoning, outsourcing can be a pleasant and beneficial venture for both the outsourcing firm and your company. In the long run, the Information Systems personnel will have career opportunities that may never have been imagined until outsourcing became a reality. Take your time throughout the entire process, don't skip any steps, develop good sound business strategies, do not lose sight of the original objectives, and perhaps you too can reap the benefits of outsourcing your Information Systems organization that so many companies are enjoying.

Appendix A

Glossary

The following definitions represent the meaning of terms used throughout this book. While other definitions may be found for the same term, the definitions herein apply only to this book.

ACD — Automated Call Distribution — An automated software feature for telephone, or telecommunication, switches to route and statistically track incoming calls. The Automated Call Distribution performs five functions:

1. It will recognize and answer an incoming call
2. It will look in its database for instructions on what to do with that call
3. Based on these instructions, it will send the call to a recording
4. It will send the call to the operator
5. Use as a tool to collect cost, at the telephone number level, and consolidate the costs as needed

CEO — Chief Executive Officer — The highest-ranking executive in a firm or company. Reports to the Board of Directors and is usually very involved in the outsourcing effort.

CIO — Chief Information Officer — The highest-ranking Information Systems executive in a company. Generally reports to the Chief Executive Officer or President. The Chief Information Officer is responsible for the overall success of Information Technology and Information Systems throughout a company.

CPU — Central Processing Unit — The part of a computer that controls all the other parts. The CPU retrieves instructions from memory and decodes them. This may cause it to transfer data to or from memory to activate peripherals to perform input or output, execute a batch program, etc.

CPI — Consumer Price Index — An index used to measure inflation. The Consumer Price Index is based on all urban consumers, United States city average for all items (1982–1984 = 100), as published by the Bureau of Labor Standards of the Department of Labor.

DASD — Direct Access Storage Device — IBM terminology for a disk drive, in contrast with a tape drive which is a sequential access drive. When referring to the amount of hard disk space, it is commonly called DASD regardless of the manufacturer of the product.

FTEE — Full Time Equivalent Employee — This acronym represents staff levels in terms of full-time employees. For example, two part-time employees who work 20 hours per week are equivalent to one full-time employee working 40 hours per week. The outsourcing firm would represent these two employees as one Full-Time Equivalent Employee.

IS — Information Systems — An organization of computer-related professionals who are responsible for all aspects of Information Technology within a company. The responsibilities include data and voice communications, application programming, local and wide area networking, desktop applications and hardware, help desk, technical training, etc.

IT — Information Technology — The technology related to an organization's Information Systems infrastructure and the overall Information Systems organization.

ITC — Information Technology Council — Made up of members of the executive staff from both your company and the outsourcing firm. The Information Technology Council is responsible for ensuring that major issues are resolved before they become significant problems. The Information Technology Council is also responsible for assisting in establishing a long-range strategic technology direction for your company. In addition, the Information Technology Council is responsible for ensuring that the relationship maintains the enthusiasm and focus that was intended when the partnership began.

LAN — Local Area Network — A data communications network which is geographically limited (typically to a one-mile radius) allowing easy interconnection of terminals, microprocessors, and computers within adjacent buildings. Because the network is known to cover only a small area, optimizations can be made in the network signal protocols that permit data rates up to and exceeding 100 Mb/s. Local Area Networks are needed for client/server computing.

Outsourcing Account Team — The Information Systems professionals from the outsourcing firm who are assigned to your company on a full-time or part-time basis.

Outsourcing Team — The group of individuals from your company who are assigned the task of assessing the viability of outsourcing, developing a request for proposal, selecting the proper outsourcing firm, and structuring and negotiating the final agreement with the outsourcing firm.

P & L — Profit and Loss — A financial statement that details a company's profits and losses over a given period of time.

PBX — Private Branch Exchange — A telephone system operating within a company. A single branch exchange system is capable of providing telecommunication services to multiple locations. The locations can be in close proximity or dispersed over a wide area, i.e., several states. The Private Branch Exchange is the point that connects all internal telephones with local and long distance telephone lines.

PC— Personal Computer — A general-purpose single-user microcomputer designed to be operated by one person at a time.

Request For Proposal — A formal request for potential suppliers to quote on a specific business service as described in the Request For Proposal. The Request For Proposal normally consists of a request for pricing, services offered, timing of proposed events, etc.

Scope Creep — A condition commonly referred to when small tasks are continually added to the contract after the contract is signed. As the contract matures, more and more out-of-scope conditions will be added to, and thus increase, the overall value of the contract.

SLA — Service Level Agreement — A document describing the contractual performance measures that the outsourcing firm needs to meet. The Service Level Agreement is used to specifically identify performance measures that will determine the overall success of an outsourcing agreement.

Statement of Work — An attachment to the contract that is dedicated to the technical description of the actual work to be performed. The Statement of Work is the document in which you define the day-to-day responsibilities, performance measures, Service Level Agreements, actual hardware and software to be used, etc.

UPS — Uninterruptable Power Supply — Used to improve the effects of poor electrical power quality, including voltage anomalies, high-frequency noise, or ground loops. A UPS is especially applicable where power outages of more than a half-second duration are possible. Simply stated, the job of the Uninterruptable Power Supply is to provide clean electrical power to the mission-critical components of your technical infrastructure. In the event of an electrical power outage, the Uninterruptable Power Supply also provides power, via backup batteries, to your primary processors (mainframes, servers, etc.) in order to conduct a controlled shutdown of your systems. In doing so, the Uninterruptable Power Supply becomes a means to prevent a system crash.

WAN — Wide Area Network — A hardware and software data and voice communications system. Wide Area Networks extend over distances greater than one mile and connect users in different buildings, states, or countries. Wide Area Networks consist of multiple Local Area Networks tied together, typically using telephone company services.

Appendix B

Sample Service Level Agreement

System Services

1. Maintain a monthly average CPU interactive response time of 1.1 seconds.
2. Maintain all network servers, telephone switches, and mainframe systems with a 99% availability rate. Rate excludes scheduled 'down time'.
3. In the event of system failure, ensure that there will be no significant data loss.
4. All cabling (including fiber optics) will be kept in good working condition and adhere (at a minimum) to the standards listed below:

Cabling	Standard
Twisted Pair	Level 5
COAX	RG58AU
Fiber Optics	62.125

5. At a minimum, maintain a 60% initial call close rate. The initial call close rate is defined as the number of help desk calls that are closed during the initial phone call from the customer.
6. Enroll new network users within 1 business day from receipt of the new appropriate form.
7. Install new or move existing telephones, personal computers, and printers within 2 business days from receipt of appropriate documentation.

8. Office Moves — Within 2 weeks of request. Request includes approved floor plan layout, with phone numbers, and personal computer locations.
9. Take ownership of all calls and ensure proper handling of each call.
10. Ensure detailed call tracking records are maintained.
11. Report fax and copier problem calls to the appropriate personnel.
12. For any data collection or bar coding problem, a technician will respond (onsite) within 1 hour.

Application Services

1. Level 1
   Application services goal in responding to a help desk call is within 1 working hour. If the call leads to a more complicated solution and further analysis is required, the call becomes a level 2 call.
2. Level 2
   Defined as the analysis level, where a problem or request is being analyzed and solutions/alternatives are being defined. The customer is notified of the status change. The intent is to resolve the issue within 2 working days.
3. Level 3
   Represents that a programmer/analyst is actually working on the problem or modification. The goal is to resolve the problem within 1 to 2 weeks.
4. Level 4
   Situations in which the problem will be forwarded to the appropriate software supplier for additional assistance. The customer is notified of the status change and 48 hours thereafter of the status. The goal is to resolve the problem within 1 to 3 weeks.

Appendix C

Request for Proposal

Table of Contents

Section I — General Information for Bidders

S. Equipment that can be bid
T. Cancellation
U. Copyrights and right to data
V. Confidentiality
W. Conflict of interest
X. Contract documents
Y. Amendments to contract
Z. Communications and notices
AA. Payment for goods and services
BB. Business recovery plan

Section II — Company Background Information

A. Introduction
B. Organization
C. History

Section III — General Requirements

A. Objectives
B. Scope
C. Specifications
   1. Introduction
   2. Information Systems organization
      a. Telecommunications services
      b. System services
      c. Application services
      d. Other
6. Growth
7. Maintenance and service
8. Contracts
9. Leasing
10. Current costs/budgets

Section IV — Information Required from Bidders

A. Proposal approach
B. Business organization
C. Statement of the problem
D. Management summary
E. Proposed hardware
F. Contractor support
G. Maintenance and service
H. Cost
I. Project plan and implementation
J. Project organization and staffing
K. Additional information
L. Proposal submittal

Appendixes

Appendix D

Outsourcing Contract Outline

Article I. Agreement, Term, and Letter Agreement

1.1 Agreement
1.2 Term
1.3 Certain definitions
   a. Access
   b. Outsourcing firm software
   c. Outsourcing firm-supplier software
   d. Your company software
   e. Your company-supplier software
   f. Software
   g. Application services
   h. System Services

Article II. Services to Be Performed by Outsourcing Firm

2.1 Outsourcing firm personnel and management
   a. Outsourcing firm Account Manager
   b. Interviews and performance
   c. Transition of personnel
   d. Financial responsibility of outsourcing firm

Article III. Your Company Obligations

Article IV. Equipment and Related Agreements

Article V. Software

Article VI. Confidentiality, Security, and Audit Rights

Article VII. Payments to Outsourcing Firm

Article VIII. Dispute Resolution

Article IX. Termination

9.1 Termination for cause
9.2 Termination for nonpayment
9.3 Termination for insolvency
9.4 Termination upon sale or other disposition
9.5 Significant business change
9.6 Termination at will
9.7 Termination for failure to provide critical services
9.8 Transition services upon termination
    a. Services
    b. Charges
9.9 Recovery of costs

Article X. Outsourcing Firm Performance, Warranties, Indemnities, and Liability

10.1 Performance
10.2 Warranty disclaimer
10.3 Intellectual property indemnification
10.4 Cross indemnification
10.5 Indemnification for employee costs
10.6 Indemnification procedures
    a. Notice and control
    b. Settlement
10.7 Limitation of liability
10.8 Contractual statute of limitations
10.9 Acknowledgment

Article XI. Miscellaneous

11.1 Right of outsourcing firm to engage in other activities
11.2 Binding nature and assignment
11.3 Notices
11.4 Relationship of parties
11.5 Hiring of employees

Statement of Work

3.1 Service description
     3.1.1 Long distance voice and data services
     3.1.2 End-user desktop support
     3.1.3 Services
3.2 Resources
     3.2.1 Equipment
     3.2.2 Staff
3.3 End-user training
3.4 Roles and responsibilities
3.5 Deliverables
3.6 Performance measures
4.0 Manage voice communications services
4.1 Service description
4.2 Resources
     4.2.1 Equipment
     4.2.2 Staff
4.3 End-user training
4.4 Roles and responsibilities
4.5 Deliverables
4.6 Performance measures
5.0 Manage application development and support
5.1 Service description
5.2 Resources
     5.2.1 Equipment
     5.2.2 Staff
5.3 End-user training
5.4 Roles and responsibilities
5.5 Deliverables
5.6 Performance measures

Attachment A — Hardware and Equipment

Attachment B — Staffing Plan

Attachment C — Hours of Staffing

Attachment D — Service Levels

Attachment E — Your Company-Retained Expenses

Appendix E

The Disaster of an Improperly Managed Partnership

For illustration purposes, the actual company's name or outsourcing firm's name is not important. Therefore, I will refer to the company as the American Manufacturing Company (AMC) and the International Outsourcing Services (IOS) firm. Any resemblance of companies names in the case study to actual companies with the same name or acronym is purely coincidental and not intended.

The Company

The American Manufacturing Company is a medium-sized company with several subsidiaries. It is a privately held company with sales of approximately $500 million and employs approximately 2500 employees worldwide. The manufacturing environment at American Manufacturing Company is a mixed mode environment where a portion of the manufacturing facilities run in a discrete manufacturing (many product features and options depending on the market and specific customer mix) environment, while other parts of the company are operating within a repetitive manufacturing, or continuous, environment. American Manufacturing Company's market is highly competitive and absolutely relies on having the products at the right place at the right time in order to meet the demand of their customers.

As a predominantly make-to-stock company, American Manufacturing Company has a nationwide distribution network that drives the demand for the majority of the company's products. The large majority of American Manufacturing Company's customers orders are received via telephone calls to order entry personnel. The remaining customer orders are received via fax, electronic data interchange (EDI), and mail. American Manufacturing Company's business is further complicated by the fact that the manufacturing facility for the majority of products was in an "out of capacity" situation. As a result, the large majority of products that are developed could be sold immediately.

The company runs the manufacturing facilities on a 24 hours a day, 7 days a week basis. Since many of the operations and material management business processes are highly automated, tools provided by the Information Systems organization are heavily relied upon. The business processes include:

- Taking customer orders
- Scheduling the production floor
- Ensuring raw materials are ordered in a timely fashion
- Timely and accurate production reporting is performed
- Packing slips generated
- Shipping notices sent
- Shipping product to distribution centers and customers
- Receiving payments
- Paying supplier invoices

The above are all very critical, or mission-essential, processes for the company. A breakdown in any one of these areas would definitely result in lost sales and lost profits.

The Information Systems organization at American Manufacturing Company consisted of approximately 25 employees who were responsible for all voice, data, and imaging processing. The processing environment was centralized and accessed via a 1500 node wide area network spanning facilities across the United States with remote dial-up capabilities throughout the world. For the most part, the business systems were interactive, state-of-the-market systems that were used throughout the company.

American Manufacturing Company also had a fairly sophisticated user base. The majority of the employees were highly skilled on the existing computer system and pursuing ways to constantly improve their utilization of the system. The relationship between the Information Systems personnel and the user base was very positive and professionally rewarding for both the Information Systems personnel as well as the majority of the users.

American Manufacturing Company's Chief Information Officer was very focused on achieving the highest possible quality of services to the American

Manufacturing Company user community, management team, and shareholders. He was also committed to providing the tools necessary to achieve the strategic business plan in the most cost-effective manner. As with any Chief Information Officer, he was always looking for ways to improve the services and reduce costs. As a result, the Chief Information Officer started evaluating the feasibility of outsourcing.

The Outsourcing Process

The Chief Information Officer's decision to evaluate the feasibility of outsourcing was derived by reviewing American Manufacturing Company's current position, as it related to providing improved products and services to American Manufacturing Company's customers, and improving the overall business processes within the company. He knew that he had achieved his previous goal of establishing an Information Technology infrastructure that was capable of supporting American Manufacturing Company for the foreseeable future. As a result, he diverted his attention to the continuing improvement of American Manufacturing Company's business processes while maintaining the integrity of the Information Technology infrastructure.

Upon considering the potential benefits of outsourcing, the Chief Information Officer was convinced that the process of evaluating outsourcing would, at the very least, benefit American Manufacturing Company by asking potential outsourcing firms for their suggestions for methods to improve American Manufacturing Company's systems environment. The theory was that by recognizing outsourcing firms as the experts in the Information Technology field, the Chief Information Officer would receive valuable information on various ways to improve systems and services for his company. This alone was considered enough of a benefit to justify the time it would take to assess the feasibility of outsourcing.

The Chief Information Officer also decided to focus on three goals that he expected to realize in the event the company decided to outsource Information Systems.

1. Achieve an overall cost reduction of at least 10% over a 10-year period.
2. Improve Information Systems-related products and services for American Manufacturing Company employees, customers, and suppliers.
3. Create professionally rewarding career paths for American Manufacturing Company's Information Systems organization personnel.

The Chief Information Officer developed the business case and presented his recommendations to American Manufacturing Company's Chief Executive Officer.

Upon reviewing the Chief Information Officer's recommendations, the Chief Executive Officer agreed to proceed with the task of the Chief Information Officer evaluating the feasibility of outsourcing Information Systems for American Manufacturing Company. With this approval, the Chief Information Officer started the first steps of the outsourcing process. The Chief Information Officer began the process by discreetly identifying the top four outsourcing firms that he felt would be qualified for his company. The top five candidates were selected by:

1. Their presence in the marketplace and areas of specialization
2. Reputation of repeated superior performance as rated by independent agencies
3. Stock performance (if publicly held)
4. Specific success working with manufacturing companies
5. Overall ability to provide outsourcing services for all areas within Information Systems

After reviewing approximately 10 different outsourcing firms, the Chief Information Officer narrowed the field, based on the areas identified above, to what he considered the top five outsourcing companies, as of that point in time, that would best fit American Manufacturing Company's overall needs.

The Chief Information Officer then visited with each of the outsourcing firms and presented the American Manufacturing Company's current situation and goals for the future. It was through this process that the Chief Information Officer realized that outsourcing would be a viable alternative for American Manufacturing Company. The outsourcing firms presented a very convincing case that demonstrated the various ways that American Manufacturing Company would benefit from outsourcing. Each of the five companies focused on its core strengths and abilities to become a viable business partner with American Manufacturing Company.

After informing the Chief Executive Officer of his findings and recommendations, the Chief Information Officer was given the approval to continue the process. The approval was to continue the process up to and including defining the detailed costs and benefits and first draft of a contract with the selected outsourcing firm. The approval also included giving the

Chief Information Officer the authority to discreetly form a small evaluation team of individuals to assist the Chief Information Officer with the details needed to perform the above tasks. To create the outsourcing evaluation team, the Chief Information Officer selected his Application Development Manager, Telecommunications Manager, and American Manufacturing Company's Controller and Attorney.

The evaluation team proceeded to conduct an exhaustive evaluation of the outsourcing firms' abilities to meet American Manufacturing Company's specific requirements and fit into the overall corporate culture. During the same time the various outsourcing firms worked closely with the evaluation team to assist in deciding the appropriate scope of the outsourcing agreement and to assess the overall business potential with American Manufacturing Company. As the Chief Information Officer suspected, it did not take long for one of the outsourcing firms to rise above its competition. As a result, the Chief Information Officer and the Evaluation Team selected the International Outsourcing Services firm as their outsourcing provider of choice.

Upon presenting the final agreement, with associated costs and benefits, to the Board of Directors, the partnership was approved without condition. The board members were excited about the possibilities that the new partnership with International Outsourcing Services could bring to American Manufacturing Company.

The Outsourcing Firm

The selected outsourcing firm was a major outsourcing services provider that had many highly successful outsourcing engagements. International Outsourcing Services was an internationally famous outsourcing firm that literally pioneered the Information Technology outsourcing industry. There was no question that regardless of what American Manufacturing Company would like to do in the future, International Outsourcing Services had highly skilled personnel within its organization who would have the experience necessary to assist American Manufacturing Company where needed. They also had a very strong presence in their local area due to other outsourcing agreements. While it was not in the initial plan, the outsourcing firm did have a data center within close proximity of American Manufacturing Company's corporate headquarters. This was also thought of as an advantage since American Manufacturing Company was planning to eventually move the data processing facilities to the outsourcing firm's data center. During the outsourcing process American Manufacturing Company did a very thorough job of evaluating the qualifications for the outsourcing firm to meet their requirements. Site visits were conducted on several existing accounts, which resulted in very favorable references for the outsourcing firm.

Due to the large size of the outsourcing firm, American Manufacturing Company was also impressed by the amount of procurement power International Outsourcing Services demonstrated when it came to hardware and software purchases. International Outsourcing Services also had developed an international data networking infrastructure that was considered one of the best in the world. International Outsourcing Services further demonstrated a keen awareness of future technologies and their applicability to American Manufacturing Company's business. There was no question that International Outsourcing Services was qualified.

During the proposal phase of the outsourcing process, International Outsourcing Services was the highest bidder. While they were the highest bidder that American Manufacturing Company was evaluating, International Outsourcing Services was still considered cost competitive. The real decision was based on the one thing on which many relationships are based: trust. The chemistry between International Outsourcing Services and American Manufacturing Company was very good. Both companies felt comfortable with each other and both demonstrated the qualities one looks for when searching for a business partnership.

The Contract

The contract that was negotiated was an eight-year agreement with an estimated savings of $28 million over the total eight-year time frame. The agreement stated that the personnel would remain on American Manufacturing Company's property and that as of the contract effective date, International Outsourcing Services would be responsible for providing all services required to maintain the Information Systems environment at American Manufacturing Company.

The scope of the agreement was to transition the entire Information Systems organization excluding the Chief Information Officer (per the request of the Chief Executive Officer) and one of the Chief Information Officer's staff members. Also included in the scope of the agreement would be all systems responsibilities including:

- Telecommunications (voice and data)
- Business applications support
- Physical Information Technology infrastructure
- Help desk support
- Information Systems training for the entire company
- Local area network and wide area network management
- Mainframe operations
- Application development and support
- Engineering systems management

The agreement would be effective on the first day of the following month and all Information Systems personnel would transition to the outsourcing firm on the first day of the contract.

The Transition

In all, the transition took approximately three months to complete. This was primarily due to the contracts that American Manufacturing Company had with various hardware and software companies that had to be legally assigned to the outsourcing firm. In addition, International Outsourcing Services wanted to add a couple of key positions to the organization from existing International Outsourcing Services personnel.

The Chief Information Officer decided early in the process not to inform the Information Systems personnel about the pending outsourcing agreement. The Chief Information Officer felt the news would be disruptive to the normal Information Systems operations, and he did not wish to place his staff in this turmoil until he was certain it was going to happen. Once the contract had been signed by both his company and the outsourcing firm, he informed the Information Systems personnel of the decision to outsource. As discussed in the text, the Information Systems personnel went through the full range of the SARA (Surprise, Acceptance, Anger, Reconciliation) model. Since the Chief Information Officer had a good deal of time to contemplate the reactions of his organization, he felt he had a good understanding of how his organization would react to the news.

The Information Systems personnel reacted as expected, with the entire staff being upset and angry about the newly formed partnership with the outsourcing firm. Within a matter of a few weeks the majority of the Information

Systems personnel accepted the decision and gave the Chief Information Officer their full support. However, to the Chief Information Officer's surprise, a few staff members never did accept the situation and eventually left the company before the transition took place. This was surprising because the individuals who were the most upset were the ones who stood to gain the most professionally from the agreement with the outsourcing firm. Unfortunately, they did not stay with American Manufacturing Company to find this out for themselves. By the time the contract was actually signed, the Information Systems personnel who were still with American Manufacturing Company were excited and eager to get started with International Outsourcing Services.

The Chief Information Officer spent many weeks prior to the transition preparing American Manufacturing Company for the eventual change. As a result, American Manufacturing Company was well informed and had the proper expectations for the transition. The most difficult part of the transition was the time required for the International Outsourcing Services Account Manager to come up to speed on American Manufacturing Company's processing environment and overall business issues. It also took some time for the Information Systems personnel to fully appreciate the qualifications of the International Outsourcing Services Account Manager and because of this, it took a while to build a good professional rapport.

Overall, the transition was uneventful. International Outsourcing Services brought in a transitioning team that specialized in transitioning employees from their existing companies to International Outsourcing Services. International Outsourcing Services also made every effort to ensure the user community and management team of American Manufacturing Company were well informed of the process and that the overall transition would be seamless as far as the rest of the company was concerned. International Outsourcing Services was correct. The transition went flawlessly, and the outsourcing agreement was off to a great beginning.

The First Six Months

After the initial transition, the Chief Information Officer and the International Outsourcing Services Account Manager established a set of performance measures, in accordance with the guidelines specified in the contract, upon which the outsourcing firm and the overall success of the partnership would be measured. These measures were collectively defined, and it was agreed that they would be updated on a monthly basis. Other tasks were also agreed upon between the Account Manager and the Chief Information Officer. Examples of the tasks upon which they reached agreement included:

1. Procedures for reporting problems with systems
2. Providing the physical and data security required for the new Outsourcing Team members
3. Establishing the level of authority the Account Manager will have during normal operations
4. Establishing the level of authority the Account Manager will have during system emergency situations, such as mainframe computer failures, network outages, telecommunications outages, etc.

The International Outsourcing Services Account Manager also spent a great deal of time working with the Chief Information Officer to assist in understanding the detailed methodologies employed by the outsourcing firm for things such as system evaluations, development efforts, requirements definition, project methodologies, etc. This was very helpful for the Chief Information Officer because it gave him an opportunity to understand the detailed process that the Information Systems personnel would be learning and expected to comply with after the transition to International Outsourcing Services.

The Chief Information Officer expended a great deal of effort ensuring that the rest of the American Manufacturing Company organization was kept aware of the status of the newly formed partnership and the progress that the outsourcing firm was making with American Manufacturing Company. The Chief Information Officer was especially concerned about the level of acceptance of the outsourcing firm within the executive ranks of the company. While the corporate executives were dedicated and supported the decision to outsource, there were many operations management personnel who were opposed, for various reasons, to the newly formed partnership with the outsourcing firm. As a result, the Chief Information Officer spent the majority of his time promoting the efforts of the outsourcing firm and the benefits they brought to American Manufacturing Company on an ongoing basis. The Chief Information Officer realized that without the buy-in and acceptance of the operations executive team, the likelihood of success for the outsourcing firm was very low.

After the initial transition, the International Outsourcing Services Account Manager started evaluating the current systems environment at American Manufacturing Company. This evaluation included all business applications, operations infrastructure, telecommunications, and adminis-tration software (i.e., word processing, spreadsheet, graphic presentations, etc.). The intent was to establish a baseline of the current systems being utilized and their overall effectiveness throughout American Manufacturing Company's organization. The result of the evaluation was a detailed list of issues as well as potential areas for improvement.

During the same time the Account Manager was conducting the systems review, he was also evaluating the skills of the Information Systems personnel that transitioned to International Outsourcing Services. In addition, he was filling several key positions with employees from International Outsourcing Services that understood the International Outsourcing Services organization and could assist in the overall training and management of the account for International Outsourcing Services.

The results of the skills assessment were favorable. All employees were found to be skilled in the areas for which the Account Manager felt he needed the assistance. The Information Systems organization, as a whole, was reor-ganized to align with the approach that the Account Manager wanted to take in supporting American Manufacturing Company. The majority of the Infor-mation Systems personnel agreed with the new approach. Those who did not agree resigned their positions with IOS and were replaced by personnel of equal or greater technical skills. Those who stayed with IOS went through a career development exercise that identified goals for each of the Information Systems employees and future potential opportunities.

It was clear that after a very emotional transition and time of uncertainty, the Information Systems employees were now settling in with their new company and enjoying a new-found interest in their careers and the fact that they were now working with a company that specialized in Information Technology as opposed to manufacturing. The Information Systems person-nel discovered that the career opportunities with IOS were endless. They also understood that high achievers in the outsourcing firm were personnel who dedicated themselves to their jobs and put their best effort forward in all tasks they performed. What was once thought of as the worst thing that could ever happen to them was quickly becoming one of the most positive events to happen to them in their careers. The Chief Information Officer felt very good about the accomplishments the company had made and the fact that he could see the favorable results of his decision and the long process asso-ciated with outsourcing Information Systems.

At that time, the Chief Information Officer and the Account Manager collectively established a priority list which identified the higher payback opportunities as top priorities. As one of the top priorities, it was decided that conducting a business process re-engineering (BPR) effort for one of American Manufacturing Company's business units would result in significant improvement in reducing costs in areas such as warranty, scrap, rework, premium freight, and labor efficiencies. The Chief Information Officer and the Account Manager then developed a plan for conducting the business process re-engineering review for that specific business unit. The plan was presented to the executive staff, who unanimously agreed with the approach, timing, and overall need and associated benefits.

Once the systems evaluation and personnel skills assessment were completed, the Account Manager turned his attention to addressing the priorities as established by the Chief Information Officer and himself. One of the first items they targeted was to launch the business process re-engineering for one of the business units. In order to accomplish this, the Account Manager determined he needed additional skills to help coordinate and manage the overall process. As a result, he arranged to have a couple of IOS's business process re-engineering specialists assigned to his team to support this effort. Per the agreement in the contract, the Chief Information Officer had the right to approve anyone from the outsourcing firm prior to their being assigned to the American Manufacturing Company account. The personnel the Account Manager wanted to use for the business process re-engineering effort were interviewed and approved by the Chief Information Officer. The Chief Information Officer felt that the personnel had the qualifications needed to get the job done.

A project plan was developed with the business process re-engineering team and presented to the business unit management team. The plan was also presented to the executive management of the business unit as well as the corporate executive management team. All parties agreed with the approach, scope, and timing of the project.

As all this was occurring, the Chief Information Officer and the Account Manager continued to build their relationship through establishing trust and respect for each other's capabilities and strengths. It was a very positive time for both parties and for both companies as a whole.

The First Sign of Trouble

Everything was going so well that it did not seem possible that the partnership was headed for some major problems. The Chief Information Officer and the outsourcing firm's Account Manager knew that a very common problem with outsourcing is the resistance-to-change monster that always appears when anyone starts to implement new ideas or business process changes. As a result, the Chief Information Officer and Account Manager were constantly reviewing the status of each change and continuing to promote the entire program across American Manufacturing Company. They both knew it was just a matter of time before they would encounter a problem related to the resistance to change.

It took approximately four months before they started to see isolated instances related to the resistance to change. The Chief Information Officer and the Account Manager resolved the large majority of the issues by working with the individuals and getting them involved in order to make them part of the solution rather than victims of the imminent change. They also ensured them that the actions being taken were in the best interests of American Manufacturing Company and the individual's specific area of responsibilities.

One of the primary individuals resistant to change was one of the executives within the business unit for which the business process re-engineering project was being conducted. Once this executive realized the business process re-engineering team was going to be suggesting that his area should change the way it does business, the executive was admittedly opposed to the overall effort. The business process re-engineering team knew they were now facing a significant issue. To complicate matters further, neither the Chief Information Officer, Account Manager, nor the business process re-engineering team leaders did not receive the support necessary from the higher-ranking officials in the company to overcome this obstacle.

As a result, the business process re-engineering effort was eventually canceled and viewed as a total failure. While it is a common fact that many business process re-engineering projects do not succeed, this was a classic example of one of the biggest reasons why they don't — the fear of change and lack of senior management support. The failure of the business process review team was a significant blow to the newly formed partnership. While the Chief Information Officer and Account Manager were disappointed in the outcome of this event, they knew that if they continued to properly manage the partnership that time would heal the wound.

Around the same time the business process re-engineering team was closing down the project, American Manufacturing Company's Chief Executive Officer announced that the Board of Directors was in the process of selling the company. To say the least, the Chief Information Officer and Account Manager were concerned about this announcement and started to think about the long-term effect this would have on the partnership. While he never shared the thought with the outsourcing firm's Account Manager, the Chief Information Officer had a sinking feeling that this was the beginning of the end for the relationship between American Manufacturing Company and IOS. With the company going through the acquisition process, it was understandable that the Chief Executive Officer's priorities were clear. They were focused on the sale of the company and not the success of the outsourcing effort. The Chief Information Officer understood and accepted this fact.

The Chief Information Officer's Role

As time went by, the Chief Information Officer tried repeatedly to gain the attention of the Chief Executive Officer in order to better define the Chief Information Officer's overall role in the sale of the company and his role for the future. The Chief Information Officer also continued to discuss, with the Chief Executive Officer, the problems American Manufacturing Company was having with the outsourcing firm stemming from the lack of support for the outsourcing initiative within the American Manufacturing Company organization.

During the entire outsourcing process, the Chief Information Officer was focused on achieving the best possible agreement with the outsourcing firm and ensuring that American Manufacturing Company was making the right decision for the right reasons. One of the issues the Chief Information Officer addressed with the Chief Executive Officer was the change in focus that the Chief Information Officer would be taking after the Information Systems organization transition to the outsourcing firm. While the Chief Information Officer brought this to the Chief Executive Officer's attention on numerous occasions, there was never any clear direction given by the Chief Executive Officer as to what role the Chief Information Officer would play in the future for American Manufacturing Company.

As a result, after the transition was completed, the Chief Information Officer found that after spending over a year dedicating large amounts of time and energy to the outsourcing process, he suddenly had a very large void in his daily responsibilities. This resulted in a large amount of time that should have been directed toward other meaningful activities within American Manufacturing Company. What ensued was a very depressing and slow time for the Chief Information Officer who viewed himself as a person who just accomplished a very significant task resulting in millions of dollars in savings for his company. To say the least, this was the beginning of a downward spiral for the Chief Information Officer within American Manufacturing Company. This was due to the lack of commitment from the executive staff and was coupled with the fact that the Chief Information Officer was unsuccessful in having a new role defined for him. With the lack of support from the Chief Executive Officer, combined with the failure to define the Chief Information Officer's future role with American Manufacturing Company, the Chief Information Officer decided to resign his position at American Manufacturing Company.

The Account Manager

All things considered, the outsourcing firm's Account Manager did an excellent job in keeping his staff together and informed. Since he and the Chief Information Officer worked so well together, the Account Manager was concerned when the Chief Information Officer resigned.

During this time of turmoil, for reasons unknown, the International Outsourcing Services Account Manager was directed by his superiors to start marketing within American Manufacturing Company for new business. With the absence of the Chief Information Officer, the Account Manager was temporarily requested to report to the Chief Executive Officer. While this may be viewed as a positive move in the eyes of the outsourcing firm, in reality it was a very awkward position for the Account Manager. With the sale of the company still pending, the odds of the Chief Executive Officer having time to manage the partnership between American Manufacturing Company and International Outsourcing Services was very remote. The Chief Executive Officer had a much higher priority to focus on. As a result, the Account Manager had no guidance from American Manufacturing Company and was left to manage the business without any support from the executive staff of American Manufacturing Company.

Daily Mode of Operation

To say the least, with a company in the process of being sold and the loss of the Chief Information Officer, the partnership between American Manufacturing Company and International Outsourcing Services was diminishing rapidly. It became apparent that the outsourcing firm had no executive support within American Manufacturing Company. As a result, anyone who disagreed with the Account Manager or any member of the Outsourcing Team, knew that he could go around the stated policies and circumvent anything the Account Manager was doing. Since the International Outsourcing Services Account Manager had no one to oversee his performance, the outsourcing firm personnel stopped tracking the performance measures as initially established by the Chief Information Officer and the Account Manager. This was not the fault of the Account Manager, as he knew that even if he were to continue to collect the performance measures, no one at American Manufacturing Company would be reviewing them.

In addition to the already strained state of the partnership, various managers within American Manufacturing Company were trying to provide direction to the outsourcing Account Manager. While the intent was good, the directions often conflicted, leaving the Account Manager to determine which set of directions he and his team should follow. This eventually sent the wrong message to American Manufacturing Company and the outsourcing Information Systems personnel. As a result of this and everything else that was happening, the Information Systems personnel became very disillusioned with the overall environment and suffered a significant blow to morale as a whole. To say the least, this had a significantly negative effect on overall productivity and the progress of projects that were under way.

Even through the chaos that had been established, the outsourcing Account Manager was able to keep his Outsourcing Team in a somewhat positive state and was able to achieve the minimum goals as stated in the contract. At this point in time it became a matter of survival. The Account Manager knew that in order to keep from defaulting on the terms of the contract, he and his team had to perform. This was quite an accomplishment given the circumstances and demonstrated why the outsourcing firm was one of the leaders in its field. They were committed to doing everything in their power to save the relationship with AMC. This included performing tasks that went far beyond the scope of the contract.

The Final Results

After going through several months in this mode, it became apparent that the outsourcing firm was not going to be given the leadership necessary within American Manufacturing Company to make the partnership a long-lasting one. The American Manufacturing Company management team, having now successfully completed the sale of the company, was in a dilemma. The company that acquired American Manufacturing Company was not very fond of outsourcing Information Systems services. As a result, the resistance to the outsourcing Account Manager grew stronger. The American Manufacturing Company management team was in a quandary since the contract with the outsourcing firm was now beginning its second year and there were significant penalties for terminating the contract without cause. However, even with the knowledge of this penalty it was clear that it was inevitable that the relationship was not going to survive.

Understanding the inevitable, the International Outsourcing Services Information Systems personnel started looking for positions with other companies. Most of the employees were concerned about their longevity with both American Manufacturing Company and the outsourcing firm. As a result, a few of the employees left the company, while others decided to stay the course and see how things would unfold. As one could imagine, the Information Systems employees had very little motivation and started questioning their loyalty to both American Manufacturing Company and International Outsourcing Services. All this just made a bad situation worse.

After a total of two years of trying to make the partnership work, American Manufacturing Company terminated the contract with International Outsourcing Services. This was done after a great deal of money was spent with International Outsourcing Services, and none of the projected benefits were achieved.

What Went Wrong

There is no question that throughout the initial outsourcing process and during the first six months of the contract, the partnership was being well managed and had the potential of being a successful venture for both American Manufacturing Company and International Outsourcing Services. What happened after that is a classic example of what happens to partnerships that are not effectively managed. There were many people who tried to blame the fact that American Manufacturing Company was being acquired during the first twelve months of the outsourcing agreement as the primary reason for the failed partnership. However, this was not the case. There is no business reason why the partnership could not have survived the fact that American Manufacturing Company was being acquired by another company. Regardless of who the parent company of American Manufacturing Company was, the Information Systems required to run the business would still be a necessary function. If the partnership was being managed properly, it could not only have survived the sale of the company but could have made the acquisition a much smoother process than it actually ended up being.

There were many things that occurred that one could say contributed to the eventual failure of the partnership. I believe there were five primary reasons for the eventual demise of the partnership. The five areas were:

1. Not knowing what to do with the Chief Information Officer after the outsourcing contract was signed
2. Lack of executive support from American Manufacturing Company
3. The outsourcing firm executive management did not become involved in the partnership until it was too late
4. The outsourcing firm was unable to obtain the personnel with the right skill mix in the time frame in which they needed them
5. American Manufacturing Company did not assign someone to take the Chief Information Officer's place, or assume his responsibilities, when he resigned

Let's take a look at each of the five areas and determine what exactly occurred and what could have been done to prevent the problem from occurring in the first place.

1. Not Knowing What to Do With the Chief Information Officer After the Outsourcing Contract Was Signed

Upon completing contract negotiations and the transition process, American Manufacturing Company did not proactively reassign the Chief Information Officer in terms of adding responsibilities for him to manage. As in any professional position, it is critical that the position remain challenging and professionally rewarding. Once the outsourcing process was completed, the Chief Information Officer found he had extra time on his hands. While I am sure the change of pace was enjoyable for a short period of time, it was an environment that the Chief Information Officer was very concerned about. After several months of this slow pace and nonrewarding environment, the Chief Information Officer became disenchanted with his position.

It should have been realized that the Chief Information Officer had just completed a major project that few Chief Information Officers have the opportunity to do. While the Chief Information Officer appreciated having the opportunity to go through the outsourcing process, he realized that once the process was completed his professional career would drastically change at American Manufacturing Company. What he was not prepared for was the indecision and large area of uncertainty that followed.

Realistically, it is natural for someone who has just completed a major project to expect a calm period. Also, after completing a project that would net the company several millions of dollars in savings and had a great deal of visibility from the Board of Directors and throughout the organization, one would know that it would be a difficult act to follow. Realizing this, the Chief Information Officer knew there would be a period of adjustment after the transition to the outsourcing firm. The six months that followed the transition were spent working with the outsourcing firm's Account Manager in establishing the guidelines in daily operation procedures. This was necessary to ensure that the partnership would be managed in an effective manner on an ongoing basis.

The business relationship between the Chief Information Officer and the outsourcing Account Manager was going well and the outsourcing firm was performing up to expectations. But this was not enough. The Chief Information Officer knew that in order for him to remain satisfied with his level of contribution to American Manufacturing Company, he would have to gain additional responsibilities. The duties required to maintain the business partnership with Information Outsourcing Company was not requiring all of his time; he needed additional value-added tasks to remain professionally challenged. After numerous attempts to convince the Chief Executive Officer that he needed additional responsibilities, he eventually gave up and assumed that things would not get any better for him at American Manufacturing Company.

As a result, the Chief Information Officer lost faith in the American Manufacturing Company organization and ultimately the pride in the position that he held. The fact that the Chief Information Officer eventually resigned from American Manufacturing Company was an inevitable and predictable action for an executive management team member who is suddenly found to be ineffective in his position.

The Chief Executive Officer should have been ready for the inevitable fact that the Chief Information Officer's daily activities were significantly reduced in terms of the amount of time required to manage the overall Information

Systems organization. The Chief Executive Officer could have ensured that additional meaningful responsibilities would be assigned to the Chief Information Officer.

If the intent of the American Manufacturing Company's Chief Executive Officer was to eventually replace the Chief Information Officer or to eliminate the Chief Information Officer position entirely, then the Chief Information Officer should have been informed and included the elimination of his own position during the transition process with the outsourcing firm. As any Chief Information Officer knows, when going through the outsourcing process, there is a strong probability that the Chief Information Officer's job will be eliminated, or significantly redefined. As a result, American Manufacturing Company's Chief Information Officer was prepared to accept that fact and do what was necessary in the best interest of American Manufacturing Company.

2. Lack of Executive Support from American Manufacturing Company

During the business process re-engineering project led by the outsourcing firm, the team started running into problems related to the resistance to change. The executive in charge of the business unit was supportive of the project during the introduction and project start-up. This quickly changed, however, when the team started making suggestions for improvement that involved business processes in his specific area. The executive was persistent and eventually successful in stopping the whole project. During this time, the American Manufacturing Company executive management team did nothing to support the business process re-engineering project team and allowed the single executive to continue to push for the demise of the project.

The Chief Information Officer made numerous attempts to gain the attention of the Chief Executive Officer. He was not successful because the Chief Executive Officer stated that it was up to the Chief Information Officer to resolve this issue and that because of the sale of the company, he did not have time to spend on this issue. As with any business process re-engineering project, the team knew that all of their ideas and suggestions would not be implemented. What they did not expect was to have the entire project closed down because of one individual who did not want to change or be a team player.

The American Manufacturing Company's executive team should have intervened when the business process re-engineering team started to run into problems with the business unit executive. Instead, the project team, Chief Information Officer, and the outsourcing firm's Account Manager were left to resolve the issues without assistance from anyone else at American Manufacturing Company. Clearly, this is the best approach to take until one sees that it is not working. Then the Chief Executive Officer, or his appointee, is expected to assist in resolving the issue.

3. The Outsourcing Firm Executive Management Did Not Become Involved in the Partnership Until It Was Too Late

During the outsourcing process the executive management of International Outsourcing Services was involved and committed to closing the contract negotiations and establishing the partnership. However, after the initial transition the executive management team of International Outsourcing Services was not as involved as they should have been in the partnership with American Manufacturing Company. During the outsourcing process both American Manufacturing Company and International Outsourcing Services agreed to implement the Information Technology Council, which consisted of executive team members from American Manufacturing Company, as well as International Outsourcing Services. A significant event such as American Manufacturing Company being sold or the Chief Information Officer resigning should have been an automatic trigger for the Information Technology Council members to meet. This was not the case at American Manufacturing Company. The International Outsourcing Services Account Manager was keeping his immediate supervisor informed of the day-to-day issues and concerns at American Manufacturing Company, but the Information Technology Council was never called to a meeting. In addition, the executive team of International Outsourcing Services never came in to try to resolve any issues with American Manufacturing Company. As a result, the International Outsourcing Services Account Manager was left to try to salvage a partnership — an impossible task for someone at his level.

When the Chief Information Officer resigned and when American Manufacturing Company announced that the company was going to be acquired, both American Manufacturing Company and International Outsourcing Services should have called a meeting of the Information Technology Council. In this meeting a strategic plan could have been developed to ensure that International Outsourcing Services was part of the process of the acquisition and not a victim of it. One would also think that the executive management of International Outsourcing Services would have scheduled meetings with the executive management of American Manufacturing Company to negotiate an understanding of how International Outsourcing Services could assist American Manufacturing Company during the acquisition process.

4. The Outsourcing Firm Was Unable to Obtain the Personnel With the Right Skill Mix in the Time Frame in which They Needed Them

While things appeared to be going well for the first six months, there were some issues with the International Outsourcing Services Account Manager in providing the personnel with the skills needed to improve American Manufacturing Company's operating efficiencies. While there were several individuals assigned from other parts of International Outsourcing Services to work on the American Manufacturing Company account, there were others who were needed but were never assigned. Many believed that this was the beginning of the end for the American Manufacturing Company and International Outsourcing Services partnership. In the minds of many American Manufacturing Company employees, this left a bad impression about the outsourcing firm, since during the outsourcing process International Outsourcing Services was very confident that the skills needed would be found and assigned to American Manufacturing Company within a relatively short time. Regardless of the reasons, it did not happen and as a result, left a bad impression of International Outsourcing Services on many executive team members of American Manufacturing Company.

What should have happened is the personnel who were promised to American Manufacturing Company should have been allocated to the account on a temporary basis, if nothing else. Doing so would have shown the American Manufacturing Company executive team and its employees that the outsourcing firm did, in fact, live up to its promises and provided the high-quality services for which the firm was world famous.

5. American Manufacturing Company Did Not Assign Someone to Take the Chief Information Officer's Place, or Assume His Responsibilities, When He Resigned

Upon receiving the resignation of the Chief Information Officer, American Manufacturing Company's Chief Executive Officer did not assign the responsibility for managing the partnership with the outsourcing firm to someone else. Instead the Chief Executive Officer assumed the responsibility himself. In doing so, he assumed that he would have the time to manage the partnership. Since he was heavily involved in the sale of the company, it was highly unlikely he would have the time to effectively manage this partnership.

Upon the Chief Information Officer leaving American Manufacturing Company, the responsibility of managing the partnership with the outsourcing firm should have been assigned to an executive team member other than the Chief Executive Officer. Since the Chief Executive Officer was heavily involved in the acquisition, it was not feasible that he would have the time to spend on managing the partnership to the level of detail that would be required. It is also highly likely that by assigning the responsibility to another executive team member would have potentially saved the partnership with the outsourcing firm. It would also have been realistic to think that, if the outsourcing firm and American Manufacturing Company partnership had been properly managed, International Outsourcing Services and American Manufacturing Company could have found a way to have the outsourcing firm assist in the acquisition process as well as improve the daily operations of American Manufacturing Company.

Any one of the above problems is a potential disaster for managing partnerships between your company and an outsourcing firm. The five issues combined is a formula for failure. There is no way that the partnership could have survived under the circumstances they were given. It is unfortunate, because all five of the issues could have been avoided. This does not mean that it would have been easy, but failure certainly could have been avoided by having the insight and desire to make the partnership last.

How to Avoid the Disaster of Mismanaging a Partnership

Given the events stated above, it was almost as though the partnership between American Manufacturing Company and International Outsourcing Services was doomed from the beginning. But this did not have to happen. If the proper steps had been taken in a timely fashion, the partnership could have been strong and long lasting. To avoid falling into the same traps that American Manufacturing Company and International Outsourcing Services did takes a great deal of focus and attention by both the outsourcing firm and your company. No one can assume anything, and everyone must do his part in continuously improving and strengthening the relationship between the two companies. To avoid these and other potential issues requires a great deal of dedication and professional management by both the outsourcing firm and your company. You must adhere to strict policies and guidelines that must be placed in your company.

It is also essential to have the Information Technology Council meet on a regular basis to not only address the technical direction for your company, but to ensure that the relationship between the two companies is as strong as possible. Let's face it, when we talk about a partnership in outsourcing, it is in both parties' best interest to ensure that the partnership is a successful one. There are no winners in a partnership that does not work.

Index